PRAISE FOR *CHECKING IN*

"I spent years with Michelle Williams when she was a member of Destiny's Child and in the years since. I never knew that she was suffering with depression. It shows how deceptive depression can be! I am proud of her for writing about it. I could not put this book down, because it was so informative in dispelling many of the myths and stereotypes that stop us from seeking the help and support that we need. Michelle has written from the heart, with great humor and love. The chapters are interwoven with her unabashed honesty and some entertaining stories about her journey, and 'the crash' that changed her life. A must-read."

—TINA KNOWLES LAWSON, COFOUNDER OF WACO
THEATER CENTER, AUTHOR, AND PHILANTHROPIST

"Tenitra Michelle is doing God's work by simply telling her story. She is inspiring millions of people to not only do the work on themselves but also teaching us how to show up for others. As a person who has lost friends to suicide, there is nothing worse than asking yourself over and over Why didn't I check in more? Oftentimes the person who needs to be checked on is closed off and this book is giving us the tools to keep compassionately checking in."

—LENARD "CHARLAMAGNE THA GOD" MCKELVEY,
NEW YORK TIMES BESTSELLING AUTHOR, MULTIMEDIA MOGUL,
AND FOUNDER OF THE MENTAL WEALTH ALLIANCE

"Michelle Williams is unlike anyone else I know. She's completely real and tells it like it is, all while making you laugh. Her book, Checking In, is a lifeline to anyone struggling with anxiety or depression."

—BOB GOFF, *NEW YORK TIMES* BESTSELLING AUTHOR
OF *LOVE DOES* AND *EVERYBODY, ALWAYS*

"In my many years practicing psychiatry, I've come to realize that depression can affect anyone at any time, and when it does, they seek understanding and advice for getting through it and finding joy again. Michelle Williams's Checking In cuts through the stigma around mental health and shows readers that it's okay to ask for help. Inviting readers to honestly face their pain by checking in with God, themselves, and others, Michelle is courageous and shows readers that they, too, can begin to walk in freedom."

—DANIEL AMEN, MD, FOUNDER AND CEO OF AMEN CLINICS

"As someone who has struggled with severe depression, trauma, and anxiety, I am so grateful for the candid way Michelle talks about her battle with depression. With raw vulnerability, Michelle courageously meets readers right in their own pain and lets them know that they're not alone. Checking In is a beautiful read—a gentle, funny, and practical guide for anyone who is ready to embrace the journey toward wholeness."

—TANA AMEN, VICE PRESIDENT OF AMEN CLINICS
AND *NEW YORK TIMES* BESTSELLING AUTHOR

"A wonderful testament to the resilience of the human mind, and to how powerful hope and love can be."

—DR. CAROLINE LEAF, NEUROSCIENTIST AND
NEW YORK TIMES BESTSELLING AUTHOR

"Michelle Williams is one of the bravest, strongest women I know. She has fought through very public struggles and dark, hidden days of depression. And now, in Checking In, she's putting it all out there for everyone to see. Her story is powerful and relatable, and she wants you to know that you are not alone. Healing is possible. And she's here to walk through it with you."

—SARAH JAKES ROBERTS, FOUNDER OF WOMAN EVOLVE, COPASTOR
OF THE POTTER'S HOUSE, AND AUTHOR OF *WOMAN EVOLVE*

CHECKING IN

CHECKING IN

*How Getting Real About Depression Saved
My Life—and Can Save Yours*

Michelle Williams

WITH HOLLY CRAWSHAW

NELSON
BOOKS

An Imprint of Thomas Nelson

Published in Nashville, Tennessee, by Nelson Books, an imprint of Thomas Nelson. Nelson Books and Thomas Nelson are registered trademarks of HarperCollins Christian Publishing, Inc.

Author was represented by the literary agency of The Fedd Agency, Inc., P. O. Box 341973, Austin, Texas 78734.

Thomas Nelson titles may be purchased in bulk for educational, business, fundraising, or sales promotional use. For information, please email SpecialMarkets@ThomasNelson.com.

Unless otherwise noted, Scripture quotations are taken from the Amplified® Bible (AMP). Copyright © 2015 by The Lockman Foundation. Used by permission. www.lockman.org

Scripture quotations marked NIrV are taken from the Holy Bible, New International Reader's Version®, NIrV®. Copyright © 1995, 1996, 1998, 2014 by Biblica, Inc.® Used by permission of Zondervan. All rights reserved worldwide. www.Zondervan.com. The "NIrV" and "New International Reader's Version" are trademarks registered in the United States Patent and Trademark Office by Biblica, Inc.®

Scripture quotations marked NIV are taken from The Holy Bible, New International Version®, NIV®. Copyright © 1973, 1978, 1984, 2011 by Biblica, Inc.® Used by permission of Zondervan. All rights reserved worldwide. www.Zondervan.com. The "NIV" and "New International Version" are trademarks registered in the United States Patent and Trademark Office by Biblica, Inc.®

Any internet addresses, phone numbers, or company or product information printed in this book are offered as a resource and are not intended in any way to be or to imply an endorsement by Thomas Nelson, nor does Thomas Nelson vouch for the existence, content, or services of these sites, phone numbers, companies, or products beyond the life of this book.

ISBN 978-1-4002-2334-3 (eBook)
ISBN 978-1-4002-2333-6 (HC)
ISBN 978-1-4002-3065-5 (ITPE)
ISBN 978-1-4002-3094-5 (Signed)
ISBN 978-0-3101-3056-7 (Custom)

Library of Congress Cataloging-in-Publication Data

Names: Williams, Michelle (Tenitra Michelle) author.
Title: Checking in : how getting real about depression saved my life-and can save yours / Michelle Williams.
Description: Nashville : Thomas Nelson, 2021. | Includes bibliographical references. | Summary: "Acclaimed musical artist Michelle Williams shares the intimate, never-before-told story of how, even in the midst of enormous fame and success, she battled depression, leading her to find her true calling as an advocate for mental health--especially her own"-- Provided by publisher.
Identifiers: LCCN 2020042612 (print) | LCCN 2020042613 (ebook) | ISBN 9781400223336 (hardcover) | ISBN 9781400223343 (epub)
Subjects: LCSH: WIlliams, Michelle, 1979- | Singers--United States--Biography. | Depressed persons-- United States--Biography.
Classification: LCC ML420.W55205 A3 2021 (print) | LCC ML420.W55205 (ebook) | DDC 782.25/4092 [B]--dc23
LC record available at https://lccn.loc.gov/2020042612
LC ebook record available at https://lccn.loc.gov/2020042613

Printed in the United States of America

21 22 23 24 25 LSC 10 9 8 7 6 5 4 3 2 1

I'd love to dedicate this book to my father,
Dennis M. Williams III. I know where I get the strength and
will to always get up and fight. I got that from you, Dad. Even
though you're not with me on earth, the legacy you left me is!

I'd also like to dedicate this book to those who are
willing to go through this journey of transformation.
Belief in yourself and God will be restored!

Contents

Introduction

HAVE YOU EVER BEEN IN A ROOM THAT WAS completely dark? Not a ray of light or a shred of sunshine to grab on to?

Even if it's just for a handful of breaths, darkness is an otherworldly experience, isn't it? It feels . . . off. A little panicky. Your hand searches the wall for the light switch with a heck of a lot more urgency than when you can see.

You may be able to take a few steps in any direction, but even the familiar becomes a stranger in the dark.

In July 2018 I was swimming in a sea of darkness.

And I mean it was darker than dark. I was untethered. A hundred miles out into the middle of the ocean on a moonless night with no sign of help.

But this wasn't physical darkness. No flip of a switch or pull of a string was going to bathe me in the relief of light. Because I was in emotional and spiritual darkness—buried beneath the bricks of anxiety and depression.

What songs will they sing at my funeral? I wondered, already judging their choices.

I just knew that this time, the darkness was going to swallow me right up.

I found myself imagining the entire service. Fantasizing about it. Debating which scripture should be read. I didn't list any family members as singing or speaking, because I thought that'd be too much to ask.

I went as far as writing down my requests:

- All white flowers.
- Invitation only.
- Private open-casket viewing prior to service.
- Closed-casket service, because I don't want people to be trying to take my picture to send to TMZ or some other nonsense.

(Looking back, that's a pretty solid list, actually. I'd stick to it today.)

And like everybody who's ever thought about their funeral, I wondered who'd show up. Which of my friends, family, and *duh*, which of my exes would sit on pews and mourn the loss of me?

I joke with you, but I was dead serious.

While I do think everybody should give their loved ones an idea of how they'd like to be celebrated after they're gone, my thoughts had gotten too graphic. My mind had gone too far.

I didn't have an exact plan for how I'd end my life, but those thoughts were quickly forming.

And I was so ashamed.

I'd been talking publicly about my struggle with mental illness for more than a decade, but nobody knew how bad it had really gotten. My platform was about the depression I'd had "in the past." I had stopped talking about what was going on with *me*. Current me. Now me.

I had stopped checking in, so I was preparing to check out.

Somehow—only God can explain how—I picked up the phone.

"I don't feel safe." Then I said the strongest three words a person can say: "I need help."

And that's the short version of how I ended up checking into a mental health facility under a false name with my lip hair grown out to my chin and smelling like I hadn't showered in days (because I hadn't).

I checked myself into a hospital because I wasn't checking in anywhere else.

I wasn't checking in with me. I wasn't checking in with God. And I sure wasn't checking in with others.

Since then, I've been passionate about sharing what I've learned—what I'm *still* learning—about the importance of checking in.

Now Michelle, you're thinking, *what are you even talking about? Checking in? Is that some clinical term or recovery phrase?* Maybe—I don't know. All I can tell you is that I had to come up with some sort of process that would keep me healthy for the days when I struggle more than others, and for the long term.

Here's how I see it (in no particular order. All three of these practices work together for the best result—the best *you*):

- **Check in with God.** I know what you're thinking: *Well, duh. We should always be checking in with God.* But I'm not talking about the on-the-go prayers we pray in a knee-jerk way, though there's nothing wrong with those. I'm talking about carving out consistent time to be gut-level with God. Because until we start talking to him regularly in an honest, sometimes R-rated way, our check-ins with God will be on the surface. When we can look at ourselves and say, "God, I acknowledge we've got a hot mess over here, but I know you can help fix it," then we will see life change and freedom.

I checked myself into a hospital because I wasn't checking in anywhere else.

- **Check in with you.** Sometimes this is the hardest habit to get into. We're busy, we're tired, and when we get a minute alone, we want to check *out*, not in. But this step matters. Because we can't be honest with anybody until we've been honest with ourselves. We have to get in the habit of looking in the mirror and asking tough questions. Heck, take yourself on a date! Put it on the family calendar. And we've got to be kind to ourselves. Some of us are walking around cussing ourselves up one side and down the other. We wouldn't be friends with somebody who talked to us the way we talk to ourselves!

- **Check in with others.** This one has become so incredibly important to me. If it weren't for that person picking up the phone that summer day in 2018, I literally don't know what would have happened to me. The people I checked in with the night before I checked myself into a mental health center were a pastor friend and his wife. I had cultivated a relationship with them over time that made me feel safe enough to tell them the truth—the whole truth. They prayed with me. They said they loved me and didn't judge me. They told me that if I needed help, I should get it. And fast.

That conversation gave me the courage to make another call, to my therapist. She helped me find a center to check into. Checking in with those people may have saved my life.

We need honest, real, vulnerable relationships. And we can't expect them to fall in our laps. We have to nurture and grow them. And sometimes, we have to seek out people whose lives look the way we'd like ours to look. You usually hear about pursuing people in dating. But the same goes for friendships! Healthy people can add value to our lives, and we shouldn't be afraid to pursue those people as friends. Then, in turn, we can add that same value to others' lives.

These three practices don't come naturally to me. I'm a very private person and don't open up to anyone easily. And even though I still have a ways to go, I'm more content, more confident, more *me*, and freer than ever.

I pray this book you're holding reveals to you the grueling lessons I had to learn about staying checked in—with myself, with God, and with a handful of healthy people who love me enough to tell me the truth.

Can we consider this book one long check-in? If so, keep reading. Because I'm holding nothing back.

Chapter One

THE FIRST THING I DO WHEN I CHECK IN AT A HOTEL is look at their room service menu. I don't need Egyptian cotton sheets or turn-down service, and I don't even travel with my own fancy pillow. But I do enjoy some quality room service. I will critique an entire establishment based solely on what they have on their room service menu. No grilled cheese or peanut butter and jelly sandwich? I immediately judge the entire establishment.

Listen, hotels, we're out traveling. We're not in our homes, so we're gonna need our comfort foods. I don't want to look at your menu and see nothing but arugula and mixed pears and goat cheese. I want to see macaroni and cheese, biscuits, stuff with butter all over it. I want hot dogs and a nice, tall glass of lemonade by the pool, not a piece of lettuce wrapped around a piece of lettuce. Mmkay?

Believe it or not, the Four Seasons hotel in New York City has the *best*—my mouth is watering just thinking about it—*the* best toasted peanut butter and jelly sandwich. I've tried to recreate it, and it cannot be done. If you were to give me the choice between a nicely cooked ribeye steak or that toasted PB&J, I'd choose the PB&J *all day*.

Like most of you, not all my experiences checking into a hotel have been amazing. I remember the first time I had a professional gig singing backup for a recording artist on tour. This is when I learned about the "A crew" and the "B crew." If you're on the artist's A crew, you stay in the five-star hotel where the artist stays. And if you're on the B crew, you stay somewhere else—somewhere that's not a five-star hotel.

Now, let me say that I totally get this. When you're touring with a hundred-person team and moving them from city to city, there's a budget that has to be managed. But this one particular check-in was bad; actually, it was the worst hotel check-in of my entire life.

It was before my Destiny's Child days, and I was touring with an artist on their B crew, staying with some of the other backup singers and dancers. We were all just getting to our rooms when I heard a person screeching down the hallway. We all ran toward the noise and quickly understood what it was about.

Y'all, there was actual human poop sitting on top of the toilet seat. I don't want to gross you out by going into detail, but it was enough poop to know for sure the housekeeping staff hadn't been inside that room since the last guest—much less had anyone squirted the first spray of disinfectant.

Honey, we raised so much hell after that check-in, we about brought the roof down.

I'm not a diva, despite the full-hair-and-make-up Michelle Williams you're used to seeing on stage or TV. I'm actually not high maintenance, but my OCD cleaning at hotels is real. To this day I take my Clorox wipes to any place I check into, and I wipe down all the surfaces. And if I'm checking into somewhere for more than a few nights, I'll swing by the store and pick up some Scrubbing Bubbles, some Lysol, and a sponge too. That's when I'll really get to work.

Recently I stayed in a luxury hotel in Los Angeles for a couple of weeks, and the shower had this beautiful gray slate tile flooring. I got out my sponge and cleaner, and by the time I was done, that gray tile was beige.

Don't hear me saying the service staff at these places don't work hard, because I know they do. But they're turning over the rooms so quickly, they don't have time to get all the dirt and grime off the shower floors. I'm not mad at them. But I'm also trying not to live in constant discomfort and anxiety after checking in.

Here's my point: it takes a certain amount of personal effort to create a check-in experience that's good for our hearts. Can't nobody else know exactly what we need to say, do, or scrub to create a peaceful place for us to rest.

I didn't always know this. Nope. There were a lot of sleepless and uncomfortable nights before I figured it out. These realizations came slowly and, in many instances, painfully. They came after I was in one of the most successful girl groups of all time, after I got engaged, after that engagement fell apart, and after *I* fell apart.

But let me back up.

I want to tell you about this one hotel I am in love with. When I check in there, I am never ready to check out. The hotel is located on a little island tucked away in the most beautiful clear waters. The sun is always shining, there's a constant light breeze, and the air carries the sweetest scent that's just the right combination of lavender, jasmine, and lemon verbena.

Now, let me tell you about the accommodations at this hotel. As far as food goes, they serve their trademark brownies around the clock. First of all, they're complimentary. Second of all, they're made with dark chocolate and hand-whipped cream cheese. Available at midnight? Check. Contains cheese *and* chocolate? Check. Check. And even though these brownies taste so indulgent that you feel like you need to apologize to somebody for eating them, they have absolutely zero calories.

This place just makes me happy, and it's more than the brownies. The natives on the island are so friendly and inviting and eager to help too. They are just good folks. You know the kind I'm talking about—people you can trust no matter what. They don't hurt people, lie to people, or do people wrong. And wouldn't you know it, but I'm a better person there too! I never lose my temper, respond out of insecurity, or pop off when I feel backed into a corner.

But the single most important quality of this hotel that I love so much is that when I'm there, I am always satisfied. There is no disappointment, shame, or regret. Depression? Anxiety? None for me. And the natives there don't even know the meaning of those words.

By now you're probably like, *Michelle, drop a name, a pin, or a GPS coordinate. A place where everyone acts right and everything goes my way? This hotel sounds too good to be true!*

And . . . you'd be absolutely correct. It is too good to be true.

(Come on. You knew that was coming, right?)

There isn't a hotel, motel, or Holiday Inn like this on planet Earth. And if there were, you can guarantee they couldn't drag your girl off the premises without a fight. It's what the Bible tells us heaven will be like: a place without pain, rejection, or loss.

To some degree, we are all looking for heaven on earth, aren't we? Where we and the people we love could live without all of the hard and challenging parts of being human?

But the Bible tells us flat out that we are living in a world of tribulation, distress, and suffering (John 16:33). And we're over here scratching our heads when we get disappointed like it's surprising to us or something. (Or is that just me?!)

Nope. Welcome to life. Things don't always go our way. Bad things do happen. And if we're not owning the responsibility to "check in" the right way, the bad things can make us forget all the awesome things God has done for us already. In fact, if God stopped doing for me today, he's already done more than enough to earn my loyalty and love. He has been all in my business—in the best way—from the very beginning. That has been so clear in my singing career.

There are people who are born knowing they were made to sing and people who work their entire lives to get just one of the many opportunities I've had, but growing up, I never really had a desire to be a professional singer. That's not to say I didn't bust my tail when I got the chance to sing, but I did have a lot of "right place, right time, right people" moments.

I wasn't that little girl singing to the mirror into a hairbrush and pretending I was filming a music video. For me, the idea was so out of reach that it never crossed my mind when adults would ask, "What do you want to be when you grow up?"

So after high school, I enrolled at Illinois State University to major in criminal justice. I wanted to work in law, maybe as a prosecuting attorney, a forensic analyst, or a forensic psychologist—something where I'd get to investigate crimes and murders.

I still think I would have been a good prosecuting attorney because I know how to interrogate people. I know if people are lying. I can sense it. That's my personality—to peel the onion back layer by layer until I get to the core of something or someone. That's probably one of the reasons I'm single. (It's okay to laugh. I laughed when I wrote it!)

It wasn't that I didn't sing growing up. I did. I was in the church choir and in chorus at school. But it wasn't until I was in about seventh or eighth grade that I realized my voice had some power behind it. I was at a concert with my school chorus group, and we were singing "Reach Out and Touch" at a church in Rockford called Macedonia Baptist Church. And right smack in the middle of the song, I felt the presence of God come over me, and he kind of assured me that, *man, I can kind of sing a little bit.*

As far as my family was concerned, singing professionally or commercially in a non-church setting was not really an option. I have three siblings: an older brother and two sisters, one older and one younger. My parents wanted all of us to get a good education, then get a job with insurance and benefits, and singing wasn't a viable way to do that.

But by the time I got to college, I was getting more and more invitations to showcase my voice outside of church. I was probably eighteen or nineteen years old by the time I realized that maybe, just maybe, I could do this musical entertainer thing on a bigger scale. It happened when I was in my second year at Illinois State and was invited to join a popular secular group. (*Secular.* I hate that word. There's such a negative connotation attached to it, and that's a shame because it's just the easier way to say "non-faith-based" group. But that's what it was. A secular R&B group.)

I was like, "Oh my gosh, no! I can't do that. I can't be singing about men and sex!" Or whatever they were singing about. It was a decent opportunity too. The lead singer had just left the group because she'd gotten her big record deal, and they wanted me to replace her. But I didn't do it because I was too scared of what everybody would think of me being in a *secular* R&B group.

The next year, a friend of mine called and told me he was playing keyboards for an R&B singer by the name of Monica. Maybe you've heard of her? The Grammy-Award–winning singer, songwriter, and actress—*that* Monica. This was in 1999, a year after Monica's chart-blistering album *The Boy Is Mine* was released.

So I told my friend, "Well, if she needs a background singer, I'm down." I wasn't going to let another opportunity pass me by.

He called me not too long after that and said, "Hey, she's having auditions tomorrow in Atlanta. Can you get here?"

And I was like, "Man, I can't afford no next-day ticket." So my friend reached out to a family member of his, Ms. Gladys, who worked for United Airlines. She got me a buddy pass to Atlanta so I could audition to be Monica's backup singer. And that's when God showed up and put me where I needed to be. (And shout-out to Ms. Gladys for helping make that happen!)

I got to Atlanta, did the audition, and landed the gig. I know it sounds cliché, but it literally happened overnight. I was a college student one day, and the next, I was a background singer for Monica and we were going on tour with 98 Degrees, a pop boy band that was blowing up everywhere. And that's how I got the opportunity to meet the girls of Destiny's Child.

As it turned out, the choreographer for Destiny's Child was also a dancer for Monica. She passed along my name to the group when they started looking for a new member. She told them I'd be a great fit. Out of nowhere, I got a phone call from Tina, Beyoncé's mom. Next thing I knew, I was on a plane to Houston to try out for the group.

And the rest, as they say, is history.

When I look back at that time in my life, I can so clearly see the fingerprint of God on the map of my journey, and it makes me wonder how I could ever fall into seasons of disconnection and doubt in my faith.

But I do. We all do. That's because a relationship with God is just that—a relationship. It needs the same care, attention, and communication as any other growing, changing relationship.

So, no, on earth, there is no mystical hotel on a remote island inhabited by saints where everything goes our way. Yes, we do live in a fallen world where people hurt themselves and each other on a daily basis. But we *can* check in with ourselves when that happens and remember all that God has already done for us.

And now you're thinking, *Duh, Michelle. I get it. Sometimes bad stuff happens. I don't expect a perfect life.*

If that's true, why do so many of us walk in despair and heartache when something painful happens to us? Why are we so quick to forget the work the Lord has already done? So ready to give in to the depression and anxiety that plagues one quarter of the people in our country?[1]

I think it's because *knowing* something can happen is not the same as it actually happening. We don't know how a certain hurt or wound will tempt us to react until we've been hurt or wounded.

To put it simply, we just ain't ready. We haven't prepared ourselves, our hearts, or our communities in a way that sets us up for success when the unavoidable happens. But maybe more importantly, we haven't grounded ourselves in what God says about us. And until we're able to base our identity on his truth, we can't know how to check in with ourselves or anyone else.

Here's a fact that probably only my OG fans know about me—my first name is not Michelle. Michelle is my middle name. My first name is actually Tenitra (Teh-nee-trah). When my career first started, there was a conversation about changing my stage name from Tenitra to

Michelle. And while I am sure everybody had the best intentions, one statement was made that really stood out to me: "Who do you think little girls want to be like? Tenitra or Michelle?"

In the moment, I was like, "Well, half the time people don't even say *Tenitra* right anyway." And this is still true! Just the other day, somebody called me Teh-night-ra. That's a new one—you have to work those letters pretty hard to wind up there.

But when it was posed to me that way, I went with it. I didn't even have a discussion about the name change out of fear because the girls and management had gone through *so* much with the member changes. They were beat up in the press and media, and I didn't want to rock the boat.

I agreed that Michelle was obviously the better label, so I started going by Michelle. And if I were to be honest with myself about the reasons why I agreed to the change, I would say it was largely rooted in fear. That has been a pattern of mine—being afraid to have the hard conversations because I don't wanna ruffle feathers or seem ungrateful for an opportunity, so I don't ask any questions.

What if I said no and lost my chance to be in Destiny's Child?

Honestly, I was afraid to disagree on pretty much anything at that point, so I accepted the new label of *Michelle*.

Don't get me wrong—there was something special about being Michelle on stage and being Tenitra to my family. It sort of felt like I could keep a little bit of myself away from the world and only give it to the people who really knew me.

And yet, looking back now, I wonder how much my feelings of unworthiness may have sprung from comments just like that one. I wonder how much influence I lost by exchanging that label.

Maybe little girls would have loved Tenitra. Because Tenitra was authentic. Because Tenitra was resilient. Tenitra bounced back. Tenitra was confident. Nothing shook that girl. Tenitra was fearless. Tenitra never doubted that she'd be successful. In fact, Tenitra was capable of almost anything.

Let me tell you a story about Tenitra that very few people know. When I was about sixteen years old, I got my driver's license. You'd have thought it was an Olympic medal, I was so proud, walking around showing it off to everybody. Problem was, my parents wouldn't let me drive. Matter of fact, my parents didn't let us do much of anything. They were the strictest parents I knew.

One Friday night, a bunch of the popular people were headed toward the neighborhood gas station. Did y'all have this? That one stop in the middle of town where everyone sort of congregated? For us, it was the old Amoco on Auburn and Central. Everybody would kind of park their cars a certain way and just hang out and chill.

At the time, I had a crush on this guy. I don't even remember his name now, but I'm sure he was bad news. And because this was long before the days of being able to stalk folks on social media, I had to get in my car and drive somewhere if I wanted to know if he was there. So I did what any resourceful teenage girl would do. I grabbed the keys to my dad's Honda Accord, and I headed out. Without his permission.

The last thing my sister said before the door closed behind me was, "You better not be taking Daddy's car."

I ignored her. The store was so close! We could walk there. I'd be there and back before anybody even knew I was gone.

So I was one stop away from the store, and it was one of those four-way intersections where everybody has a stop sign. As you might imagine, I was in a little bit of a hurry. So I did a rolling stop, paused, then accelerated. One second I was driving to the store to see my crush, and the next, the car was sitting in somebody's front lawn. I'd been hit, T-boned, actually. By a car that had blown through the intersection.

It was an out-of-body experience. To this day, I don't remember the impact.

When the wrecker got there, I told him to just take the car to my house. I was already concocting a good lie to tell my parents. *I don't know what happened to the car! Somebody must have hit it in the driveway! Can you imagine? I am just as shocked as you are!*

Unfortunately, I realized that my next-door neighbor was dating the lady whose front yard I'd ended up in. I knew he'd probably snitch on me, so as soon as the story formed in my head, I knew I'd never get away with it.

I got home, and my parents were sleeping. I decided to just get it over with, so I woke up Mama first. Immediately, she was in a panic. See, Mama had this Chrysler New Yorker she loved. It was navy blue with leather interior, had whitewall tires and a moon roof. Honey, she was *doing it big* in that car. When she realized it was not her precious New Yorker that had been wrecked, she sighed with relief.

"Well, let's wake your daddy."

My dad rose up out of that bed like an angry bear. I remember telling him, "I'll pay for it! I'll pay for it!" Which was a total joke, because I made about $130 a month. Somehow, by the grace of God, during the middle of my dad's rage, he remembered something similar he had done at my age. He was mad, but I wasn't a goner. Tenitra would live to ride another day.

But after I started performing, somehow that full-of-life Tenitra became full-of-fear Michelle. She heard time and time again that Michelle wasn't good enough. That Michelle wasn't the kind of brave and daring girl Tenitra was. That Michelle would never measure up. And she started believing it. When people say the same thing over and over again, it's hard not to hear it. It's hard not to believe it.

You couldn't tell Tenitra nothing. I'd gone to college to solve crimes and prosecute folks. But I'll never know who she would have grown up to be because I was too afraid to find out. That's not to say I wish I'd had a different career—that'd be crazy talk. But I made the decision to go by Michelle instead of Tenitra out of fear. And any time you make a decision out of fear, you risk whatever reward could have been earned from choosing courage.

If I had had the awareness to check in with myself before making that decision, maybe I would have saved myself a great deal of wounds . . . and inspired some young girls to be themselves *all the time* along the way.

See, when we fail to check in with ourselves, to be aware of our own thoughts, feelings, and spirituality, we fail to live as God wants us to live. Because we fail to see ourselves as God sees us.

One of my favorite verses in the Bible keeps me grounded. It says this:

> I will give thanks and praise to You,
> > for I am fearfully and wonderfully made;
> Wonderful are Your works,
> And my soul knows it very well.
> My frame was not hidden from You,

When we fail to check in with ourselves, to be aware of our own thoughts, feelings, and spirituality, we fail to live as God wants us to live. Because we fail to see ourselves as God sees us.

> When I was being formed in secret,
>
> And intricately and skillfully formed [as if embroidered with
>
> many colors] in the depths of the earth. (Psalm 139:14–15)

Now, let's think about this. If you spend hours making something—making anything—does it matter to you how it's received? For me, it could be something as long and drawn out as an entire musical album or as simple as dinner. If you don't like something I've made, I am disappointed. I feel like I did something wrong. I take the blame.

Now, let's think about the One who created us, God. The book of Psalms tells us that God spared no detail when he "knit" us together. The Amplified translation says we were made with such intricate detail: "as if embroidered with many colors."

I don't know if there are any seamstresses reading, but it takes me three hours to sew on a button. I just googled how long it takes to embroider something by hand, and we're talking hours upon hours upon hours for the smallest piece—and that's when you're at a professional level.[2]

The process of how we were dreamed up and planned for and loved on and created by God surpasses our ability to understand.

So when we fail to see the beauty, the perfection, the completeness of his creation—us—what are we communicating to God? What are we communicating *about* God? Basically, we're saying we know better and can do more than God can.

I mean, I know that we know that's not true. Otherwise, God wouldn't be God. But we aren't living like that's true.

We need to pay attention to *how* we're defining who we are. Because we're defined by our maker.

As a society, we value certain bags, jeans, and luggage sets not because there's anything unique about them, but because of the *who* behind the *what*. We define designer items by the designer.

I'll never forget the Dooney & Bourke bag my aunt gave me back in the day. Honey, I was taking that purse with me to the bathroom, I loved it so much. A few years later, I bought my first pair of Dolce & Gabbana jeans. I still remember what year it was: 2001. And I wore those jeans *out*. I mean, I felt fanc-aaay in them. You would have thought those jeans were out saving lives. Fighting fires. Rescuing cats from trees and keeping children safe.

And then . . . drumroll please . . . I received my first set of designer luggage. Louis Vuitton. Gorgeous. Sumptuous. To. Die. For. Miss Tina, Beyoncé's mom and one of the kindest people in the world, gifted me the set. I still have it.

If we define a bag based on its creator, why don't we define ourselves by the same standard?

The problem is, we're finding our identity in the wrong places. We're defining ourselves by the wrong labels—the labels given to us by other people or even labels given to us by ourselves. In fact, I bet if we took a stack of those "Hello, My Name Is _____" stickers, wrote down all the false labels we are believing about ourselves, and stuck them on, our entire bodies would be covered up!

Here's another question: Why don't we get more upset when we get mislabeled? Why do we just bow down and accept the incorrect labels given to us by others? It's like identity theft. And let me tell you, we will get fired up by someone trying to steal our financial identity.

Back when Destiny's Child was at its height, we'd do the craziest things to keep our identities under wraps while traveling, especially when checking into hotels. I'm not even going to play with y'all, I had fun. I'd come up with the most ridiculous fake names to check in with: Barney Rubble. Rudy Huxtable. Even now, I'm honestly nervous to put into print what my real first name is. But then I googled myself just to see how visible it already is, and my full name and photo was the first thing to pop up.

But we all want to protect our identities in certain scenarios, right? Americans spends millions of dollars a year to protect their identities.

We accept labels and hand over others without even realizing it. Because we're not checking in with ourselves, we get one false charge and we hand over the entire wallet.

I'm still single. That must mean I'm going to be single forever.

I haven't had a baby. That must mean I'm never going to be a mother.

My man left. That must mean I'm not worth loving.

We do this, don't we? We jump from point A to point Z, and we don't even question it; we don't take the time to check in and ask ourselves what's true and what's fear-based.

We even get annoyed when folks get our names mixed up with someone else's! Is that just me? Like, your boss calls you Tammy when your name is Tonya. Let me give you a recurring example from my own life.

Any *Dawson's Creek* fans reading? I never watched the show myself, but I know of friends who were obsessed with the Pacey/Dawson/Joey love triangle and the show's angsty, artsy writing. And don't even get me started on that opening number by Paula Cole. It'll be in my head for a month.

There's a celebrity whose breakout role was on that show, and her name is . . . any guesses? You got it: Michelle Williams. Now, I don't know her personally, and I'm sure she's great. She does, however, have a way of stirring the social media waters. Especially following some of her more outspoken award acceptance speeches. Michelle, if you're reading this, you do your thang, girl. We're all entitled to our own opinions. You earned the right to stand in front of that ceremonial microphone, and whatever you want to say while you're there is your prerogative.

Who I want to roll my eyes at are the many, many people who tag me in posts the morning after one of these speeches when they meant to tag the *other* Michelle Williams. I'm like this: I know the Instagram profile photos are small, but come on. I'm a tall black woman with dark hair, and the other Michelle is a cute, petite blonde. And she's white! *Open your eyes!*

If y'all are taking the time to rant or rave about a celebrity, at least make sure you're tagging the right one when you do it. Like I said, the girl has a right to her opinion. That's what makes America a beautiful place. But her opinions on certain topics contrast sharply with my own.

When my mama sees it, she's like, "Michelle, did you really say X, Y, and Z? That doesn't sound like you. Do we need to have a talk?"

No, Mama. Folks just tagging other folks with reckless abandon!

It doesn't really matter, because the people who know me know what I stand for. Still, when enough people are calling my family members and saying, "I saw on Facebook that your daughter (or sister) said this and that," they have no choice but to question. (Hey, this is for free—be careful on social media. Just be wise. Don't be a bully. Plus, some of y'all are going to get me in trouble with my mama, and I may be grown, but I still don't like to be in trouble with Mama.)

It gets to me when people mistake me for someone else. And yes, I go to great lengths to protect my identity when I feel it needs protecting. And yet, I will let this world stamp any ole label on me and I'll just take it.

That's part of why checking in with myself matters so much. I've only recently started the process of doing this regularly, and I can't tell you how it's changed the ways I've viewed myself.

The other day, I sat down with the notepad app on my phone and typed out all the false labels I had accepted over the years:

- Not good enough
- Unlovable
- Doesn't belong
- Done with music
- Unworthy
- Not pretty enough
- Boring
- Hypocrite
- Unintelligent
- Meant to be alone

I had to stop there. It was just sad. It was pitiful, really. And then I got angry. Sometimes checking in with yourself will have this result. You'll realize you've allowed too much and done too little about it.

All those labels, those awful, have-to-be-false labels, I had allowed them, and I had even embraced them. And I'd gotten so passive about it. Because I wasn't testing my thoughts. I wasn't challenging my own words. I wasn't checking in with myself.

If who I am is based on what other people say? I have no chance.

If who I am is based on the negative thoughts I have about myself? I have no hope.

If who I am is based on who made me . . . I am *his*.

The only label I've got that matters is *God's. God's creation. God's work. God's child.*

Our value as people has nothing to do with what we do, say, or accomplish. Our value comes from the One who made us: *God.*

And when we can begin basing our identity on that fact, we can begin to live more honest, meaningful, and joy-filled lives.

So I've gotten in the habit of this—of opening my phone's notepad and writing down anything I'm feeling is true about myself. Good and bad. All the labels I'm wearing. I know this sounds ridiculous, but you have to check in with your own thoughts. You may not even be aware of your own feelings.

Who am I right now? Who do others say I am? Who do I say I am?

This is the ground floor of how I check in with myself. I have to start here.

Because until you really know who you *think* you are, you can't begin to check in with yourself on a real level.

Chapter Two

LET ME TELL YOU ABOUT ONE OF MY LIFE'S LITTLE grenades that exploded because I wasn't checking in with myself.

Have you ever had someone do you dirty? (We all nod yes because duh.)

But I mean, like, have you ever had someone just *wrong* you? Betray you? I'm not talking about somebody who took your parking spot or said your dog was annoying. I'm talking about someone who yanked the rug out from beneath you. Then they rolled you up in that rug and tossed it off a cliff.

This one time I felt like I'd been literally cut. Cut so deeply that it was like slicing my finger with a sharp knife. Do you know what I'm talking about? That panicky sensation of a fresh wound? At first, you feel nothing but ice-cold numbness. You think, *Oh man. When that starts hurting, it's going to* hurt. And when the pain finally sets in, you can feel it throbbing with every beat of your heart.

Well, I've been there. And in this particular situation, it felt less like a finger slice and more like an ax in my back.

I felt betrayed. That's a strong word, I know. And in hindsight it was all probably just bad judgment on this other person's part. But at the time, babaaaay, it felt raw. It felt so personal and intentional. It rattled me like I was an old, rusty cage. I was so torn up inside that I honestly thought I was losing it.

Before we get into the details, here's my official disclaimer: the names and details of all my stories have been changed to protect the innocent . . . and the guilty.

I had a guy friend working for me whom I was very close with. Let's call him Nathan. Nathan and I were basically family. And before I hired him, I called him up. Call it woman's intuition, call it paranoia, call it whatever, but I remember calling him and just saying, "Hey, don't do me wrong. Just do right by me, and we will have a very successful working relationship. I'll be good to you."

And Nathan did a great job. He was thorough, sharp, and thoughtful. Then one day, I got an email from Nathan. Only, this email didn't come from his regular work email address; it came from *another* work email address. Like: YourLyingEmployee@YourCompetitor.com

Well that can't be right, I thought. *He works for me.*

But not only was this another work email address, it was the business of a very close friend of mine who happened to be in the same industry as me. My friend who also had no idea that Nathan was actually supposed to be working for me and just me.

Honey, I saw red. I was so hurt, so angry, so *mad*. It felt like Nathan used me to get somewhere else. Somewhere that was, in his mind at least, better and greater than working for me.

When you work in my field, you get this a lot. Users. I feel like I always have to watch my back and be on high alert for people whose intentions are less than honorable. It's exhausting.

Anyway, Nathan's actions reinforced some of my most crippling insecurities at that time—that I was just a stepping-stone to the next, better thing. And I didn't know how to deal.

So I did what you would probably do. I told my mama on him. And I remember knowing that I was a little more freaked out than the situation called for, but I was no longer in control of my reactions. I couldn't calm down. I couldn't get ahold of my thoughts, emotions, or myself. I went from raging mad to stonily silent. I paced. I couldn't sit still. My mind was racing. I cried angry tears.

I was like, "Who can we call to fix this? What's our game plan? How can we retaliate?"

Mama just looked at me. You know *the look*. The look that I could read. It said: We *ain't doing anything about this, child. You've got to handle yourself.*

My mama is an incredibly wise woman. She saw that there was something very not right with me. But instead of telling me I was acting like a crazy person, she told me as kindly but firmly as possible that it was time I went and saw a professional.

Basically, *Take some personal ownership, Michelle.* Like, *Maybe this is less of a Nathan problem and more of a Michelle one.*

At the time, I had never been to formal counseling before. Where I came from, church was your therapy. I figured only rich white people got professional help, and that wasn't me. We weren't poor or anything, but I had grown up in a very middle-class home. I didn't even know that insurance covered a good portion of each session—I was clueless.

But my mama said I needed to go, and my mama is not someone I like to cross to this day. So I went. And the direction of my life was changed forever. For one, therapy helped me avoid going to prison for assault and battery charges. And two, my counselor, Sandy, helped me see that yes, in fact, my rage over the Nathan deal had become something way bigger than it should have been. Like, my reaction should have been a 4 out of 10, and it was a 10 + 10 + 10 out of 10.

Without checking in, I had become completely unaware of myself. I was on autopilot. And the flight plan was beginning to look like a kamikaze mission.

Let me explain it this way: Have you ever had a bruise that you didn't realize you had? You banged your shin on the coffee table and just forgot about it? You don't even remember you're hurt until a little pressure is put on that same area. And then, boy oh boy, do you remember. It hurts—it stings!

I didn't know I had such a bruised heart until Nathan pressed down on my untended wounds.

And if you would have asked me how I was doing at that time, my surface answer would have been, "Fine. Okay. Just doing life over here." You know? But the truth is, I wasn't being honest with myself. I wasn't taking the time to evaluate anything on an authentically deep level. I wasn't checking in.

Sandy and I would go on to spend hundreds of hours together. But it was in that first session that I learned it was my responsibility to keep a watch on my own heart. Like, *Oh, you mean I've got to do some work to stay healthy?* Duh, Michelle. Duh.

Together, Sandy and I started digging away at the dirt of my experiences. We talked about the situation with Nathan, but it was obvious that he wasn't the real issue. The real issue was what had caused me to stop being aware of what I was feeling in the first place. When did I stop feeling like myself? When did I become a person who would fly into a fit of rage over something petty?

With Sandy's help I began excavating those hardened places I had unknowingly built around my heart. And what I uncovered was something I think I had known deep down for a while but had never been able to admit. I suffer from depression. Real, clinical, need-to-be-medicated depression.

And you might be thinking, *Excuse me? What does Michelle Williams got to be depressed about? You got a little bit of money. You got a little bit of fame. You sang in one of the most successful groups of all time.*

But one message that doesn't get shared enough is that depression can hit anybody. It hits male, female, upper-class, middle-class, lower-class, no class. Every race and every spiritual background. It can seek you out and find you anywhere, with or without "justifiable" cause. What I mean by that is that depression comes in all forms. Sometimes it's chemical. Sometimes it's genetic. Sometimes it's situational. Sometimes it's because of unmet spiritual needs. Sometimes it's because your husband left or you can't get pregnant or you got fired.

Depression is an assassin. It acts like a silent, slow killer. And if you don't deal with it, it can swallow you up.

And that's where I was the first time I walked into Sandy's office. My depression had me so disconnected, so numb, and yet, so short-fused. I was more than a train wreck; I was an earthquake waiting to happen, and everybody in my life was walking up and down my fault lines, risking receiving either my rage or my numbness with each interaction.

I remember the first time I realized there was something off with my emotions. I was in junior high school, around seventh grade. I kept feeling like something was different about me when I compared my behaviors and emotions to my friends'. I knew that I was kinda sad all the time, but I couldn't tell you the first reason why. I was isolating myself, losing interest in things I used to love, and my grades started dropping.

Classic symptoms of depression. But I didn't have a name for it. I didn't feel like I looked like a person who would be considered depressed, you know? But of course, I've learned that depression does not always have a look.

Then, in my twenties, while I was still in Destiny's Child, I remember telling someone on our team at the time, "Hey, I feel like I might be depressed." And he was like, "What do you have to be depressed about? You guys just signed a multimillion-dollar deal. You're about to go on tour. You guys are about to release your own Barbie dolls."

I mean, who gets a Barbie doll replica of themselves but can barely find the motivation to get out of bed every day?

So I thought, *Maybe I'm just tired. Maybe I'm just missing my family.*

By the time I got my actual diagnosis of clinical depression, I was thirty years old. Do I wish I had known sooner? Of course I do. But that wasn't what happened. God was still there. He knows all about depression. And no, it's not that being depressed is a sin.

Y'all should read the Bible. It's good stuff, I'm telling you. Because we're out here in the twenty-first century thinking that we invented this depression stuff, that it's a modern problem. But that's not true. Even the Bible talks about the idea of having a sound mind:

> For God did not give us a spirit of timidity or cowardice or fear, but [He has given us a spirit] of power and of love and of sound judgment and personal discipline [abilities that result in a calm, well-balanced mind and self-control]. (2 Timothy 1:7)

It's true. God has not given us a spirit of default fear, sadness, or despair. He hasn't given us a spirit of I-can't-handle-it, but-they-deserve-it, excuse-making behaviors. Those are not from God. Actually, the opposite is true. God has given us some real power through the gift of his Holy Spirit. He's given us some guidelines in his Word to help us gain some control over our thoughts, emotions, and actions. He's given us some people around us who can help. Some resources that can renew our minds and attitudes. And most of all, he's given us access to him.

Maybe your experience is a little different. Maybe you started feeling depressed after a specific event. Maybe *depressed* isn't even the term you would use, but you started feeling disconnected from things and people, including yourself.

You lost a job. Your man left. Your child was born with a diagnosis. A loved one passed away. God didn't answer your prayers the way you thought he would. Someone you looked up to disappointed you.

At some point, you stopped asking yourself the hard questions:

- Have I been letting myself feel my feelings?
- Am I withholding forgiveness from myself or others?
- What lies am I believing to be the truth?

You stopped checking in like I had.

∼

Looking back, I see my childhood as a time when I learned to cover up what was really going on. Checking in of any sort was not encouraged.

We swept everything under the rug and went about our lives as if everything and everyone was happy. I never learned how to talk about what I was feeling because no one around me did.

Oh, I could talk about God all day long. I knew Bible stories and scriptures and just about every hymn ever written—and listen, all that is so important. I don't want to downplay that. But to tell you what emotions I was experiencing? Honey, I was thirty years old before I even got started doing that.

Maybe you can relate. Maybe it's hard for you to check in with yourself because you're not even sure what that looks like. Maybe what was modeled for you by your parents was a lot like mine—we don't talk about things that might make someone uncomfortable or make someone view us or our family differently. We don't acknowledge things openly or inwardly.

Maybe your parents were the opposite and overshared. Maybe they couldn't stop talking about themselves, what they were feeling, and what they'd been through or were going through. Maybe you've gone the other direction in your own life because they were just too much. And talking about your feelings, even to yourself, is not something you want to do because your experience has been that it's too overwhelming and too hard.

I remember talking with Sandy one day early on in our sessions together. She would say, "How did that make you feel?" all the time. And my answer would always be the same: *Mad. Pissed off. Angry. Frustrated.*

Over time, she'd push me. "Why did that make you mad?"

Because they're stupid, and stupid people make me mad!

Yeah, that's me. Michelle Williams, *dream client.*

But Sandy was patient. "Think back to what happened. What thoughts did you have right before you got mad?"

That was harder to answer.

Take the Nathan situation, for example. I was so mad at him I was probably blowing smoke out my ears like a Looney Tunes character.

"What were you thinking, Tenitra?" (She always called me by my real name.)

I was thinking he's an idiot. I was thinking he's a traitor. I was thinking he is dead to me.

"Before that. What were you thinking?"

That he used me. That he didn't see me as valuable. That I was worthless, just a means to an end.

Whoa.

Okay, Ms. Sandy. I see what you did there.

This whole time, I'd been walking around with my anger, thinking I had a right to be mad. When really, I was just feeling like no one would ever see me as valuable for *me*. But I wasn't trying to be sad and wounded—being angry was much easier.

Because I wasn't being honest with myself and checking in, I had no idea that feelings of worthlessness were at the root of my anger.

I'm not Ms. Sandy, but let's just take a minute to do that exercise together. When was the last time you felt angry or sad? Think about it. Be real with yourself. What thoughts were driving that emotion?

She's just a suck-up.
Nobody appreciates me.
Nothing ever goes my way.

Now, dig a little deeper. What thoughts or beliefs are driving *those* thoughts?

I am not worth choosing.
I'll never be enough.
God has forgotten me.

You know, our thoughts draw a direct line to our emotions. We can talk ourselves into or out of just about every feeling there is. And when you're checking in with yourself like you should, you're aware of your thoughts. And when you're not, you're either angry or sad all the time, and you don't know why.

When we're checking in with ourselves, we can root out the beliefs behind our thoughts and the thoughts behind our emotions.

I wish I could tell you that this was a turning point for me, that I began checking in with my thoughts and their relationship with my emotions, but it wasn't. And like I had before Ms. Sandy, I wasted a lot more time and damaged a lot of relationships because I wasn't being honest with myself about why I felt the way I felt and why I did the things I did.

I stayed angry and distrusting.

So when I finally *did* meet a decent man, I made a 100 percent ass out of myself. That's right—a donkey's behind.

You ever do that? Look back on past behaviors and cringe a little bit? When I think of this one relationship, I automatically become that embarrassed face emoji. Like, immediately.

His name was Anthony. And let me tell you, Anthony was smooth. He was laid-back, chill, kind, and warm. Anthony was also a musician.

When we're checking in with ourselves, we can root out the beliefs behind our thoughts and the thoughts behind our emotions.

He taught himself how to play the piano and bass before he started kindergarten.

At four years old, I was over here like, "Yo, Mama. I'm gonna need some more mac and cheese while I sit on the couch watching TV and picking my nose."

Before he was a teenager, he was the director of music at a church. He had worked with some of the most famous artists of our time, and you know I tapped his shoulder on a couple of projects myself.

So there I was, dating this incredibly gifted, talented man of God who, at that point, had never given me a reason to question him or doubt him.

So what did I do?

I questioned him and doubted him, of course.

I hadn't been that way in previous relationships. In fact, I'd been a doormat with a lot of those guys. So this time, I took myself in the complete opposite direction. Way, way too far in the complete opposite direction.

I mean, I had even already had my *aha* moment with Sandy about staying in touch with the thoughts behind my feelings. But I still had a lot of learning to do, apparently, because all my good sense fell out of my head one Sunday afternoon.

We'd been dating a little while, and Anthony was in LA for work. He invited me to come visit him, so I got on a plane and flew out from Chicago, rented a car, and drove to where he was staying. Now, this was a big deal to me. It made me feel vulnerable, like I was putting myself out there by flying somewhere to see this man.

Walking up to the door, I was that nervous kind of excited—the best kind. It was like I'd traveled so far and made so much effort and I was finally getting to see my man.

So I raised my hand and knocked on the door.

Nothing.

I knocked again. Nothing. I called his phone. And still—*nothing*. Then it was like a volcano of anxiety erupted inside me. My thoughts grew arms, legs, hands, and feet and straight-up ran away from me.

Is he with another woman?
He told me to land at this time.
Was he just trying to make me look stupid?
I never get on a plane for a man.
Did he just play me?
Did I just play myself?

Furious and hurt, I gave up. And just like in the movies, right when I turned around and started walking (stomping) away, the door swung open.

There stood Anthony. A very confused, sleepy-looking Anthony. And, least-shocking news ever, he had *not* been purposefully tricking me, leading me on, or lying to me. He'd just been asleep. He'd gotten up super early and worked a long, draining day of work and had wanted to be rested when I got there.

He was napping, not cheating. (Face-palming now, years later.)

In that moment of anger, anxiety, and fear, I acted like a fool. Like, what do you say after that?

I was just teasing with all that beating on your door and hollering! Wasn't that a fun joke?! Wanna cuddle?

Nope. My relationship with Anthony was never the same. We went through the motions of having a good time on that trip, but when it was over, there was distance. He took a step back from me emotionally, which only perpetuated this new cycle of insecurity and self-doubt.

I couldn't explain to Anthony why my mind jumped from *he's not answering* to *he's being unfaithful*. Because I couldn't explain it to myself.

Heartbroken and disappointed, I (belatedly) did a little introspection. Why did I freak out? Why did I panic? There was no evidence of infidelity, so why would *that* be my first assumption?

What was the thought behind the emotion and the belief behind the thought?

I'm thinking . . . *no man will ever be faithful.*

Because I believe that . . . *everyone will always leave me.*

Now. Before you start thinking that I should moonlight as a counselor, you should know that it took me months to put those two statements into words. Months, counseling, and a lot of uncomfortable moments asking myself hard questions—hard moments of checking in.

Like all marriages, my parents went through their fair share of rocky moments. My father was a misunderstood man. I didn't relate to him because I didn't get it—but now that he's passed away, I can see it so much more clearly. I can see him so much more clearly.

Think about it this way. Let's say all of our childhoods give us an adult-functionality number of one to ten. Someone raised by great parents reaches a nine or a ten as an adult. Someone with not-so-great parents lands at the lower end.

The generation my parents were raised in was different from the one I was raised in. My grandparents had their kids in the Great Depression era—a time that was about survival. People worked as long as the sun was up, and there wasn't a big emphasis on talking with your kids or your spouse about your thoughts or feelings. You went to work, provided for your family as best you could, and you went to bed just to wake up and do it again.

That's the parenting my mom and dad were brought up with. So if their level of adult functionality was a four or five, but they parented us to be sixes or sevens, they still did more and gave more than they ever got.

But it wasn't enough. My home was not a peaceful place. It was a place where the tension stretched until it snapped, over and over again because we just didn't talk about things. There was no checking in. As a result, most of my emotional needs went unmet. I was on my own to deal with my reactions, feelings, and worries, and I was always anxious.

I worried that one day, Mama would get sick and tired of being sick and tired, and she'd leave us. As a little girl I'd sit at home, watching the clock every afternoon. My mom got off work around four, and if she wasn't home in the next half hour, the fear that she'd never come back would grow inside me with each passing second. I'd stare out the window with my heart just pounding, waiting to see her car pull into the driveway.

In my mind, I already *felt* abandoned in a thousand tiny ways, so it was only a matter of time until she abandoned me physically too.

When Anthony didn't answer his door, it triggered those places I'd never acknowledged that were emotionally deprived and expecting to be left. It was like I had brought a suitcase stuffed with unmet needs and dropped it on his doorstep and said, "Unpack these and put them away."

No man is capable of doing that. That's work *we* have to do within ourselves with the help of God.

Again, over time, not overnight, I started to learn that it's not just *today's* version of Michelle living inside this body. Seven-year-old Michelle is there with her wounds. Thirteen-year-old Michelle is there with her scars. And unless I take the time to pay attention to their hurts, we're all going to war together inside my head.

Needless to say, Anthony and I did not work out.

It took me a minute to get over that relationship. But more than the relationship, it took me a minute to get over my role—my actions—that led to our breakup. In fact, it would be years later until I fully understood my mental health's negative effect on that and other relationships.

I'll never do that again, I told myself. *Now that I know what my wounds are, I can work on them. I can be different. I will be different.*

But then I wasn't different.

Chapter Three

THERE'S THIS PICTURE OF ME WHEN I WAS LITTLE that I absolutely love.

I'm standing in front of the door of the house I grew up in just cheesing. And I may be looking all girly girl in my cute little lilac shorts and ruffle blouse with a bow in my hair, but I'm standing there looking strong. I've got my hands on my hips and my chest puffed out like, *Yeah, I'm a nice girl, but I can still take ya.*

I can't tell you how many times I've thought about the girl in that picture. How proud she was. How much belief she had in herself. How much courage.

Is it weird to y'all that I'm sometimes jealous of her—jealous of the younger version of myself? Like, how did that little girl strike the ideal balance of fierce and feminine in that picture? Some days it seems like I'm feeling every emotion God gave us all at once, and some days I worry that I'm just dead inside. How'd that girl in the photo get so emotionally dynamic?

The truth is, we can't stay young forever. We've got to grow up. I hope this isn't news to you. The thing about growing up is that none of us makes it through adulthood unwounded. Without scars. Without a story.

But, yes. There are times when I crave simpler days, the days of childhood. You know, that's one of the topics counselors and therapists love to talk about: our childhoods. And I get that. I mean, that's when we're learning the rules of life, right? That's when we're forming the basis and foundation of all our beliefs and principles.

When most people are asked to recall their earliest memory, they'll say stuff like, "Oh, my dad took me on this trip, and it was so special" or, "I had this pet that I just loved" or, "My siblings and I would always play this game together, and it always sticks out in my mind." Meaningful, sweet memories, right?

Now, if you ask my earliest childhood memory? Wait for it . . . wait for it . . .

Eating graham crackers.

That's right. Try unpacking *that* little nugget in counseling. But it's true. Growing up, I went to the Christian Life Center School in Rockford, Illinois. That's one of my earliest childhood memories: eating graham crackers there. I'd break them up into little squares and take my sweet time munching on those things. Mama didn't let us eat snacks like that at home. Only healthy, home-cooked meals. (The nerve!) So those graham crackers were the highlight of my preschool day.

I also remember snow. Profound, right? But growing up in Illinois meant snow was a significant part of my formative years. That's one of the main reasons I no longer live there; I can't stand that cold weather. But I do remember this one time my father came to pick up my siblings and me from my grandmother's house, and there was snow everywhere.

I was little enough that he picked me up, maybe because I was asleep or sleepy, and I just remember having on this huge snowsuit. I think it was one of those snowsuits with the feet sewn in so all that was sticking out was my face. I looked like a big ole bag of snow myself. I remember him picking me up and taking me to his red four-door Buick, and it was freezing. Then we were driving away, and I was looking out the window, thinking that it was all so bright and pretty.

So, yes, childhood memories for me are basically of graham crackers and snow.

Beyond those two *obvious* indicators of my solid character, I actually do remember some meaningful things, some meaningful people.

Maybe that snow memory sticks out to me because I felt safe in my dad's arms. I felt important to him, protected. I think that's the first time I had experienced that feeling of being secure and cherished.

I would spend a lot of my life seeking out that same feeling from the men I dated.

Another distinct memory I have from childhood is being in my first music class at school.

Most predictable revelation ever, right? My teacher's name was Mrs. Baker, and I have all these flashes of memories of being in her class. I remember how big the music room was and even the books we sang out of.

I remember this huge concert we sang at and all the parents clicking away on their old-school cameras. I was wearing my favorite church dress and, honey, I was feeling fanc-aaay. I was typically a little shy as a kid, but not that night. That night, I belted those hymns like I was the only kid on the stage. In hindsight, I was probably (definitely) overdoing the performance, but what can I say? Your girl loves to sing.

It was Mrs. Baker's class that kindled my passion for music. There'd been a spark before, but that class set my heart for song on fire. It was the first time I felt like I was *good* at something. It was the first time I felt like I had made my parents proud.

I came up loving music. It was the one thing I did growing up that always got me the affirmation and attention that I didn't consistently get at home. And that's not to say I was the star in every choir or anything, because that wasn't the case. But music always mattered to me—and it mattered to my family. Singing was also one of the first ways I learned to connect with God, by singing and listening to songs about him.

So when I got the unbelievable opportunity to join Destiny's Child, it was like God knew singing was meant to be my career all along, even if I didn't.

The first year of Destiny's Child was definitely a whirlwind for me. Remember, I was a college student who had every intention of graduating and getting a job in the criminal justice field. Sure, I sang a little background for an R&B artist, but I wasn't out hustling, trying to start my own thing. It was the very definition of surreal, because all of a sudden, I was a principle artist in a successful group that was touring the world. Like, *what*? I couldn't have dreamed it up.

I'll never forget my first show with Destiny's Child. We played at Shepherd's Bush Empire in London. *London*. I remember being like, *Whose life is this?* But it was mine.

I was so nervous I was sweating. Sweating everywhere. Places ladies don't sweat. Mind you, I was coming into a group that was already established. The previous members already had their individual fans, and I didn't know if I'd be ignored, applauded, booed, whatever. But I remember getting out of our car at the venue, and there were people lining the streets and I saw the first sign with my name on it. Then the second. Then the third. It was *unbelievable*. I felt loved. I felt celebrated. I felt accepted.

During my time with the group, I don't remember getting a lot of sleep. But I didn't care—I was having the time of my life. We did city after city, state after state, country after country. Matter of fact, thanks to the blessing of private jets, we did a couple of countries in one day when we were promoting an album. We were always in fittings, hair and makeup, rehearsals—I was always somewhere doing something I never dreamed was possible.

I remember my very first Grammys appearance in the year 2000. I had never been "dressed" by a designer outside of JCPenney, and I got to wear this beautiful two-piece Escada gown. It was champagne colored and, of course, coordinated with my band-mates' outfits. That was my first time on the red carpet and my first time wearing something that cost thousands of dollars. It was all very surreal, and I remember thinking how deeply, deeply blessed I was to be a part of that moment. It felt like the beginning of the rest of my life.

After that, we were off—Kelly, B, and me—traveling the world together. We were probably annoying, to be honest, always in some kind of car, van, bus, train, or plane, randomly singing harmonies together. We'd make up songs about stupid stuff, especially about food. We ate, honey. Ate, and ate, and ate.

Now I know this makes us a big olc cliché, but we were all obsessed with Popeyes chicken. In fact, we loved Popeyes so much that they gave us all Free Chicken for Life cards. I'm pretty disappointed because I don't know where that card is now. So, Popeyes, if you're reading, I ain't too proud to beg!

I think part of the charm of our time together was the beauty and depth of our friendship. We genuinely liked each other. We understood each other's boundaries. Take Kelly, for example. Kelly is a morning person. And not just like, a little bit of a morning person. Kelly is a bring-you-breakfast-in-bed-while-singing-show-tunes morning person. I don't understand this strange magic, but the girl wakes up on *go*. She's ready to get moving. Beyoncé and I, on the other hand, we need a few minutes (at least two hours) before we're capable of entertaining life in the morning.

I know the media wanted to write its own narrative of jealousy and spats and drama, but the truth is, none of that was true. I'm sure we had disagreements like any friends or coworkers do, but ultimately, we all had a deep respect for each other as artists and as women. Twenty years later, we still share that gift of friendship.

Maybe it was because of our friendship, maybe it was because of the success, but mostly I think it was just our destiny to sing and perform together. (*Destiny.* See what I did there?) I know that's true, because it never really felt like work, even though we were investing every minute, every thought, every cell of our beings into the group. Together, we just had *that thing.* That intangible, undefinable thing. *Chemistry* is a close word. All I knew at the time was I felt like I was exactly where God wanted me to be.

I'll never forget when I moved to Houston and Ms. Tina helped me set up my condo there. She fussed over getting me settled, making sure the place was furnished, painted, and decorated. She even took me to a fabric store so I could pick out the materials for my bedding and my curtains so they could all be custom made to exactly what I wanted. That was honestly such a sweet time for me. It made me miss the time when my mom would do the same for my older sisters and me—new drapes, bedding, and painting every few years. I longed for more motherly moments like that. That's not to take anything away from my own mama, but it was just a different, tender approach to helping and caring for me that I'd never experienced.

We were a family. And I think that bond is what still keeps us connected. I know the world would love for us to say we did not get along. I know the world would love to hear us bash each other or trash talk about each other in the media. Maybe that's why you picked up this book! Hoping to get some dirt on my girls. But that wasn't us. We still love each other. We still visit each other. In fact, I was with the girls just a few days ago. Our connection is real, and it's brought life to me in some of my darkest moments.

And still, even living the absolute dream I was living, with two of the most amazing women as coworkers and best friends, there would be pitch-black dark moments. It's difficult to put into words exactly what depression feels like for me. It may be completely different from how it feels for you.

Sometimes it's a numbness. It's this pervasive sense of nothing-matters-and-nothing-ever-will-really-matter that lingers in the background of every moment. When it's like that, I could sleep for a decade. And other times, it's a toe-tapping, hall-pacing anxiety that keeps me awake all night and leaves me an inch from the edge of something black and ugly.

Even during my time in Destiny's Child, it was all there—the depression. I was just too busy, too focused, too distracted to check in with those thoughts and feelings long enough to confront them. It'd be like, "Oh, depression. You're still here? Well that sucks. Gotta go do a show—we'll talk later."

Beyoncé and Kelly had no idea what I was struggling with, but that's on me. I never said a word to the two of them. I'm not even sure I had the vocabulary to say how I felt at that time.

Then, in 2005, in the same bomb-dropping fashion that I had landed my gig with Destiny's Child, it ended.

At the time, it felt like someone had detonated something nuclear in my life. But looking back, I shouldn't have been that surprised. I mean, the name of our last album was *Destiny Fulfilled*. I kind of roll my eyes at myself now. Like, if that wasn't a clear message of our direction, I don't know what was.

Logically, I could see how Kelly and Beyoncé were ready to be done. They'd been in Destiny's Child since they were nine years old—much, much longer than I had. And for them, it was a good time to end. But emotionally, I was spinning like a top. In fact, I had a hard time even believing it. Your girl was in denial. I thought, *Oh, we'll do a couple more tours. We'll do shows. This really isn't* the end. *It's just a break.*

We had taken breaks before. We had all done our own solo music while still in the group; in fact, I was the first one to put out solo music during our time together. So I couldn't comprehend the idea that we were actually finished as a group. I wasn't ready for it to be over after only six years. I had just started feeling like I belonged. It felt like the beginning of something to me. Instead, it was the end. The disappointment that followed threatened to pull me under like a riptide.

Have you ever had that happen to you? You had this master plan laid out, and all of a sudden somebody came along (life came along) and lit a match at all four corners?

Maybe you got married, but he left.

Maybe you've had your baby names picked out since middle school, but you can't conceive.

Maybe you've worked your butt off to hit that goal, but it always seems to move just out of reach.

We've all experienced this, right? Life goes left when we thought it was going right, and we catch a sucker punch that sends us reeling. And if we're not checking in the way we should be, it can quickly erode the stable ground beneath our feet.

First, let me be clear: I'm not laying blame on anyone in this scenario because no one did anything wrong. Bandmates go their separate ways all the time, and I was treated with respect and class in the dissolution of Destiny's Child. But, as is expected in anything that ends before you want it to, I was just plain sad. So everything that happened after that I viewed through a filter of hurt.

We did our last show, and everything just sort of trickled to a soul hollowing halt. When I thought about the future? Nothing. The silence I felt during that time echoed in my ears and rang louder than any note any instrument could ever play.

My natural reaction was that I needed to create new music on my own. See, while I was still with Destiny's Child, I wanted to record a gospel album. I wanted to do it at the peak of our success, because I wanted people to know that I *chose* gospel music. It was never a last resort for me.

I told Mr. Knowles my wishes and he went to work, making a dream within a dream come true. He had to have a lot of tough conversations with a lot of people to get a gospel label created. Probably his toughest sale was convincing people that even though I sang songs with the word *bootylicious* in them, I still loved the Lord. I released *Heart to Yours*. And I couldn't have done that without Mr. Knowles's connections, networking, and effort.

But eventually, leaving his management was something I felt like I needed to do. And let me tell you, that was not a favor I did for myself. I only did it because it felt right. To not have him or his company backing me was downright terrifying. Mr. Knowles is truly a brilliant mind. That whole family is just blessed with talent beyond anything I've ever seen. But it was time for me to move on, so I did. It was hard. I mean, like marathon-in-the-heat-of-summer hard.

At the time it felt like I was the only group member struggling, floundering. I did get offers, but there was no strategy, no one cheering for me consistently or steering me in a specific direction. It was like opportunity whack-a-mole—Bam! Bam! Bam!—with no rhyme, no reason, no expectation of what was going to happen next.

Then came a short time when it seemed like my career was getting back on track. Finally. I felt like I had a new direction (which at that point, would have been *any* direction). It started when I got the offer to perform in *The Color Purple*. I love theatre and always have. Matter of fact, when I was in the eighth grade, I auditioned to play Daisy Mae in *Li'l Abner*, but I didn't get the part. I was devastated. Seriously, I still get a stomachache when I think about it.

So, two years after Destiny's Child ended, getting a starring role in a nationally touring show like *The Color Purple* felt like I had come full circle. And you know what? The experience was incredible, y'all. And the show was even better. Your girl even earned a nomination for Lead Female Actress at the 2008 Eighteenth Annual NAACP Theatre Awards! I was like, *Okay, this is it. This is going to be the beginning of the next chapter of Michelle Williams's story.*

The plan was that after *The Color Purple*, I was going to do another album. But I wasn't sure I wanted to release a gospel album this time.

I remember having a conversation with my mama about what type of record I wanted to make. She said, "Tenitra, you need to do something with some *soul*. Something that people can dance to." And I was like, *If Mama says to do it, then I'd better do it.*

I decided to call the departure *Unexpected*. I knew people expected me to put out more gospel music. And I love gospel music. If you look at my playlist, that's the main genre I listen to. (Along with Afrobeat. If you've never listed to Afrobeat, do yourself a favor and check some out!) But I didn't want to do what people thought I would do. I wanted to do something different. So plans were made to release *Unexpected* in 2008.

I had actually released a second gospel record during my time with Destiny's Child, and this would be my first project since then—and the first commercial pop album I'd ever done on my own. I knew that the world would be watching how it did, and the pressure felt like I was walking around with a big ole gorilla hanging from my back. But still, I was excited. Like, *This could be it. This could be the start of what's next.*

And of course, I started getting too much in my head about it, questioning everything. *Will the gospel music community think I'm playing both sides of the industry? Will the secular music industry take me seriously as a solo artist?* Even someone without mental health issues could lose their dang mind overthinking a release with this much potential for failure or success.

Ready or not, the release was coming. And in fall 2008, my first-ever dance album dropped.

And dropped.

And dropped—down the charts.

There are a lot of tracks on that record that I still jam out to, to this day. But I may be the only one. *Unexpected* didn't do as well as I or anyone had hoped. And my music career was put on ice. Ice in the back of one of those walk-in freezers in the industry's basement.

So I thought, *I'll take the entrepreneurial route. Maybe it's time to press pause on the music, let a little time pass, and see how I feel about it.*

I remember writing in my journal that I wanted my own bath, bedding, and spa line. I made clear goals; I even wrote down what I wanted to earn after taxes. And you know what happened? I got laughed at. Literally, laughed at. I was like, "Hang on a minute. That wasn't a joke. I'm not Chris Tucker out here throwing y'all a punchline. This is what I want to do. This is my life you're cracking up about."

But they just kept laughing. Like, *Oh, honey. Keep dreaming.*

I spent a number of years after *Unexpected* feeling lost. It was like someone had dropped me in the middle of a complicated maze and told me to get out. Only they'd blindfolded me and tied my hands behind my back too. I didn't know what was happening next, and it felt like I had no one fighting for me. To this day, I sometimes have to work through those old feelings of rejection. I know everybody was doing the best they could, but at that time, I felt like I'd been abandoned.

Confused, disappointed, scared, and lonely, I withdrew into myself.

Let me tell you something about depression. Baaaby, depression loves disappointment. If you're inclined toward being depressed at all, when disappointment comes your way, depression stands up and cheers. It's like, *Yeah! This is my chance to get a foothold again!* I sat in my disappointment long enough for depression's roots to sink deep into my mind and spirit.

And I probably would have stayed there, had it not been for that little girl in the picture, that proud little girl with bows in her hair. Because even at that young age, I was being taught the right way to handle disappointment.

There's a proverb that talks about teaching a child to seek God's will:

Train up a child in the way he should go [teaching him to seek God's wisdom and will for his abilities and talents], even when he is old he will not depart from it. (Proverbs 22:6)

My parents weren't perfect, but they did what matters most: They taught me to love and fear the Lord. They taught me to seek God's wisdom and will for my life. And just like God's Word says, when I grew older, even if it took me a few failed attempts trying to do things my own way, I eventually found myself at the feet of God, begging him to take me where he wanted me.

The truth was, over time, I had allowed some distance to build between me and God. Now, I never once doubted that God was with me. I never said, "God, this is all your fault." I don't have that testimony. I do have the testimony where, because of my actions, I've run away from God. I know I have. I felt he was ashamed of me. You know how sometimes parents can be disappointed in their children? I was like, *I know God has to be disappointed in me*, and I would literally see myself spiritually crumbling and hiding from God. Over time, my actions and my choices created space between God and me.

Now, we all get to this point. A relationship with God is just like a relationship with anyone else. Sometimes you feel really close to each other and sometimes you don't. It all depends on how much time you've been spending together and how much effort you've been investing into the relationship.

The truth is, we all want to feel close to someone. We all want to feel like someone knows us and likes us. That someone is looking forward to spending time with us and cares about what we say and think. And for a lot of people, there is something really appealing about being close to God. But I know that's not the case for everybody. Maybe the idea of being close to God sounds great, but it's also kind of intimidating.

Maybe you're afraid to feel close to God. Because if you were to get honest with God and check in with God, you might hear him say something you don't want to hear. That's been the case with me almost any time I've been distant from him—shame or guilt keeps me from opening up to him. Maybe I'm afraid to hear something like, "Okay, Michelle. Now that I've got you where I want you, let me get out my list of all the ways you've screwed up lately" or, "Let me tell you all the reasons I'm mad at you." For many of us, God reminds us of an angry parent or grandparent who always finds something wrong with us. So we stay far from God.

A lot of people I know say their main fear is that getting close to God will make them miserable. In other words, the only way to be close to him is to give up everything they do that's fun.

It kinda makes me laugh, because when people who truly are close to God talk about their faith, that's never part of their narrative. They're not like, "I started checking in with God, and everything went downhill from there." But deep down, many of us still have this suspicion that there's more to the story, that being close to God is difficult and complicated. And that staying close to him is nearly impossible.

Have y'all ever heard of a guy named Abraham? He was a pretty big deal in the Bible. And his story is in its very first book, Genesis. It all starts in chapter 12, where his name wasn't actually Abraham yet, but Abram. The first thing we learn about Abram is that God showed up and spoke to him in some sort of vision or dream. He told Abram to leave the country he was living in. That may not sound like a huge deal, but it was. God basically told Abram to leave his family and everything he had ever known and go to a land that God would show him.

If it's me, I'm like, "God, I've got questions. You want me to do what? Pack up and leave my family and friends? For how long? What am I supposed to tell my mama? You know how she is. She won't understand. And wait a minute, you want me to go where? To a land you will eventually give to me? So you're asking me to be homeless in the meantime? I need details, Lord! A timeline. And a map, if possible."

But what's so interesting is that God didn't give Abram a command and then wait to see what happened next. God told Abram to leave, then God kept talking:

> "I will make you into a great nation,
>> and I will bless you;
> I will make your name great,
>> and you will be a blessing.
> I will bless those who bless you,
>> and whoever curses you I will curse;
> and all peoples on earth
>> will be blessed through you." (Genesis 12:2–3 NIV)

God was asking Abram to take a big step. But before he started, God also wanted Abram to know that there was a promise attached. He wasn't going to have Abram leave his life so that he would be miserable, but so that God could use him and give him a life Abram had never imagined. Basically, God wanted more for Abram. But Abram had to take the first step in faith, with no timelines and no guarantees of what this "better" future would look like.

Abraham's story didn't end there; it started there. Over and over God walked with Abraham and made promises, giving him bigger glimpses into the role he would play in the future of the people of God. The point wasn't to get Abraham to *do* more things. God's purpose was to continue to draw Abraham closer to himself. The point was for Abraham and God to develop a relational history together, so that when the time came and it seemed like God was asking him to do crazy things, Abraham could look back at what God had done for him already and say, "God is trustworthy. God is good. More than my obedience, God just wants me. He just wants to be close to me."

As God showed up over and over again, Abraham was learning something about God. He was learning that relationships matter to him. That God has a plan and he can be trusted. That the point for God is never to get us to do something more, but for us to get to know him better. To be closer to him.

But there's more. A lot of times when we talk about the Bible, we talk about it in two separate sections: there's the Old Testament, the part of the Bible before Jesus, and the New Testament, the part of the Bible after Jesus. I know I do this. I get so caught up in these two parts that I think the God in the Old Testament is different from the God in the New Testament. It's like, the God in the New Testament loves us and wants to be close to us. But the God in the Old Testament is low-key scary. The God in the Old Testament is kind of moody and mad. But that isn't the truth.

The story of Abraham shows us that God has always valued people; he's always valued closeness. It shows us how God has always placed the most importance on relationships, even before sending us his Son, Jesus. If anything, it was the God of the Old Testament who *did* send us Jesus. He knew that he would never be as close to us as he wanted to be unless he made a way.

So he sent his sinless Son, his perfect Son, his compassionate, strong, brilliant, and good Son to be killed. Not just to make a point. Not just so we'd follow him. Not just so we'd know he is God. He sent Jesus to make the first move—the first move toward us. To show us he wouldn't let anything stand between us. *That's* how much God wants to be near to us. It's kind of crazy, right? It's like, *Lord, you can't really love us this much? You can't really want to chill with us this badly?!*

But yes, because of Jesus, we can be close to God.

If the problem isn't God moving away from us, it must be that we're moving away from God. Because God isn't going anywhere. He doesn't take vacations to Cabo and leave somebody else in charge. He doesn't nap or get on Twitter. God always stays exactly where he is.

So how do we get close to God again after we've allowed some distance to grow between us? In the book of James, Jesus' brother put it in the simplest way: "Come close to God [with a contrite heart] and He will come close to you" (James 4:8).

Oh, is that all? You're saying that all I have to do is come to God with a contrite heart? *Contrite*—that's not a word we use a whole lot.

If the problem isn't God moving away from us, it must be that we're moving away from God. Because God isn't going anywhere.

It basically just means a heart that realizes it's in need of God. Well, honey, that's me. I know I can't face life alone, not even for five minutes.

When I realized I'd let my shame and insecurity move me away from God, I did the only thing I knew to do.

With nothing else to hold on to, run to, or rely on, I checked in with God. I said, "God, not my will, but yours. I'm tired of striving. I'm tired of fighting. I give it all up. I just want you. I just want your peace. I just want what you want—in my career, yeah. But for my entire life." I told him everything: How disappointed I was. How hurt. How pissed I was, to be honest, whether or not I had a right to be.

Now, change didn't happen right away. It didn't even happen quickly (or at least it felt that way). But the more I prayed real, honest prayers, the more I was releasing my control over my life and future, and the more I felt that vice grip of pressure loosen up a little bit. The more I felt at ease. The more I felt at *peace*. The more I felt God's presence, even when things around me weren't necessarily changing in a way I could measure.

After checking in with God regularly, being honest with him and with myself, the fog of depression slowly began to lift. Once I'd gotten over myself, gotten over my emotional reaction to the unmet expectations of the group ending, the silver linings started to peek their way through the darkness.

For one, I finally had time to take care of myself. And no, I don't mean "self-care," the term that's so trendy to talk about today, like manis and pedis, although I do get plenty of those. I mean taking care of my *heart*. Of my *soul*.

Being in Destiny's Child meant a rigorous schedule most days of the year. Kelly and Beyoncé are some of the hardest workers in the industry. All three of us performed sick, tired, and injured because we always wanted to give people a good show. It was just our work ethic.

So the group's break meant I could finally give *me* a break, even though that's the last thing I wanted.

The other obvious upside was how the group went out: on top, with grace, dignity, and friendship. You know, I still get emotional thinking about how blessed I was to be a part of something as monumental as Destiny's Child. Ending when we did and how we did left people wanting more. It's been fifteen years, and people still ask and wonder when we're going to put out new music.

It is a complete blast getting back together to surprise the world with reunion performances every now and then. It's just as entertaining for us as it is for the crowd, because we didn't get burned out, bitter, or cynical about what we had as a group.

Now, I would be lying if I said I wish we weren't still together. I would be lying if I said I didn't want to do another album. I don't know if I want to do another sixty-city tour. We ain't twenty-five anymore, you feel me? But I am going to just put this out in the atmosphere: B, Kelly, if you're reading, we could always cut a short album, maybe do a mini tour. Popeyes on me!

See, sometimes God takes away the plan of man because he wants all the glory. He wants to do it for us and in us. He wants us to make no mistake about where our help came from. He wants us to come to him. He wants us to stop praying the rote prayers that are polite and memorized. He wants us to talk to him like he's a friend. Like he's a friend who can handle our honesty. He wants us to *check in*.

Because sometimes, what you expect to happen doesn't happen. And it's not always someone's fault. Sometimes you gotta pick yourself up off the bathroom floor, wash your face, get your brows waxed, and just be honest with the One who already knows the truth.

Chapter Four

I DON'T KNOW WHAT THIS SAYS ABOUT MY TASTE in men, but my first crush growing up was the organ player at my church.

I was about five years old. He was dating my older cousin who used to babysit me. My family tells this story about how once, when she was watching me, he came to visit her. I don't remember what he was driving, but I do remember thinking it was cool, like a BMW or a motorcycle or something. And I got straight-up territorial over him! I was like, "How you gonna come visit my cousin when you know we're meant to be?"

Years later, they're happily married with kids. He's actually still a phenomenal musician and an all-around awesome guy.

And that was probably the last all-around awesome guy I had a crush on.

Y'all, I'm kidding. I really am. I've dated plenty of great men in my day, but I've also dated some men that make me look back and think, *Michelle, you are smarter than that. You knew better than that, girl.*

Nope. Not crazy. Just so critically out of touch with myself—with what I needed and deserved—that I thought it was normal to allow a man to date me without ever admitting publicly that he was dating me.

Can we take a sidebar?

This really has nothing to do with this book, so it's kinda for free. But if a man won't claim you in public, he does not deserve you in private. At the same time, if you are allowing a man to keep you in private and not demanding to be taken public, you are letting him determine your worth. There are no exceptions to these statements.

Now back to me.

In the past, if I did date men publicly, I always had a gift for finding ones who weren't ready to commit beyond that. It was like I was a magnet for those kinds of guys. Like I was holding a sign that said, "Dateable. But that's about it."

You know the guy I'm talking about. When he's with you, he's all, "Girl, you're amazing. Any guy would be lucky to lock you down." But when he's not with you, he's making zero moves to lock you down.

He's still curious. Curious about other females, other opportunities. He may not fully cross the line into "cheating," but his actions don't quite line up with his words, either.

You ever meet this guy? I've met him. A dozen times.

I've dated professional athletes, musicians, and guys with "regular" jobs, and many of them were the same. They had no issues being my man. Some were even willing to be monogamous and faithful. (How sad is it that *that* is an anomaly?) But it seemed like none of them were ever willing to take things to the next level.

I thought to myself time and time again, *What is it about me that isn't worth committing to? What am I doing wrong? Why am I not worth marrying?*

Can we pause and talk about repeating past behaviors that have hurt us? I mean, *come on, Michelle.* God has shown me time and time again that my failure to check in with myself always leads to some sort of emotional outburst that damages or ends a relationship.

I saw a quote from Hart Ramsey on Twitter this week that hit me hard. It said this: "If you don't heal properly after leaving a

God has shown me time and time again that my failure to check in with myself always leads to some sort of emotional outburst that damages or ends a relationship.

dysfunctional relationship you will end up in a different version of the same relationship you just escaped from."[1]

And I've heard quotes or sayings like this before, and I've nodded my head like, *Yeah, that's right. If you dysfunctional folks don't get it together, you're going to ruin it for the rest of us.*

It never occurred to me that I might be the one bringing the dysfunction. But honey, when you're the common denominator in all the drama, chances are you are the source of most (or all) of that drama. If your relationships with coworkers, friends, or significant others always end the same the way, that's not bad luck. That's just bad character.

So when I think back to my earliest dysfunctional relationships, I have to start at home. I think I've always had a general distrust of men. Maybe that's because my mom and dad's marriage was not the picture of love and respect. Don't get me wrong. They worked hard. They took us to church and taught us to do right. And they stayed together.

But there were times I wish they hadn't.

When my parents fought, they *fought.* It was an all-out war. I remember on multiple occasions hearing them yelling and screaming and slamming stuff all over the place, and I'd think to myself, *This is it. This is the night I'm going to have to call 911.*

One particular fight sticks out among the many.

I was probably ten or eleven years old, and my dad had been out all night on Saturday working at a club as a bouncer. The next morning, he was not in any type of mood to go to church. I agreed with him—we were always at church, and I wanted to sleep in. I don't know exactly what happened in those early hours of the morning, but what I walked in on was my mom and dad in an all-out battle.

And I was terrified.

Out of respect for my parents and their journey to where they are today, I won't go into further detail. Just know that this wasn't a cute fight. It didn't end in a truce or with an "agree-to-disagree" attitude. No, it ended badly—very badly.

And would you believe that we still went to church that Sunday? More than that, we still put on our choir robes and sang as if nothing had just happened. I remember being in the choir loft and thinking, *What the hell are we doing? Are we just going to pretend that didn't happen? Are we just going to act like our family isn't falling apart?*

But we never discussed it. There was never an, "I'm sorry y'all had to see that," or even a threat not to tell anyone what we'd seen. They knew we wouldn't tell because that was just our family's way—image over honesty.

So when I reflect, I have to start with the relationships I have with my mom and dad. I have to ask myself some tough questions:

Did your parents lay hands on you growing up?

They didn't hit us, but they didn't hug us either.

Did your parents let you go hungry?

We weren't starved for food, but we were starved for communication, empathy, and intimacy.

Did you have bad parents?

I had human parents. And instead of looking to God to get my unmet needs satisfied, I have looked to romantic relationships to do that.

When I think about that, when I really check in with that reality, I'm embarrassed. I've never seen myself as a needy person. In fact, I'm happy being alone. (Probably too happy, but that's another chapter.) I have never been a woman who has needed a man for anything. Or so I thought. But the truth of the matter is, in practice, I've relied on the men I've been in relationships with to prove to me that I am worthy.

That's a burden far too great for another human to bear.

I have a sweet friend and mentor named Donna, who has walked with me through some powerful healing. She helped me see what I was doing by explaining it to me this way:

> Imagine you have a nice, tall glass of water. That water is what you bring into a relationship for the other person to drink. But instead of pouring a fresh glass of water each time we enter a new relationship, we go back into past experiences of hurts and wounds and pick up dirty rocks and sticks, and we dump them into our glass.

Now, I admit to a little OCD. I won't drink a glass of water if there is even a *blur* on the inside of the cup. But here I was, sloshing around my brown dirt-water and begging everybody I was in a relationship with to drink it and keep it down.

Another way to say this is that *you will always repeat what you don't repair.*

I lost more than I was willing to lose before I learned this lesson. I had been letting seven-year-old Michelle dictate what happened in thirty-year-old Michelle's relationships for far too long.

I met Chad in June 2017. And, yes, Chad is Chad's real name. Yes, he's the Chad of our television show together, the man I was engaged to. He knows I'm sharing our story and said "as long as the book's not cheesy," he's cool with it.

Chad is the founder of an awesome ministry called Elevate International. I had a friend invite me to go to one of their retreats for young people, and I had a little time between projects, so I went. I didn't really know Chad or anything about him, but when I got to the event, Chad's best friend's wife started teasing me about him.

"Y'all would look so cute together," and "You should go say hey."

I was like, "No! Stop!"

But I'm not even going to play it off. I thought Chad was fine.

When I met him, he was very cordial and proper. You know, you can tell when a guy's checking you out, even on the sly, and I got zero vibes coming my way from Pastor Chad. The weekend ended up being great, and I really enjoyed my time there and had no ulterior motives when it came to him.

Right before I left, however, Chad did "have" to get my number to help with getting me a ride back to the airport. At the time, I wondered if he'd use it. Well, he did.

Chad's first text to me was, "Hey Michelle. I remember you said there were some people in Phoenix you wanted me to meet. Also, how about you and me meeting some time to connect?"

I was like, *What the heck does that mean? Connect?* Does he mean talk? Play a round of Connect Four? Go out? Arrange a business lunch? Like, you need to ask me to dinner if you really want to go to dinner. You need to ask me on a coffee *date* if you want to go on a coffee date. Spell it out for us, gentlemen. Don't play it safe. That's soft!

In true Michelle fashion, I was already reading rejection in this first communication, so I ignored him.

A couple of weeks later, I was scrolling through Instagram and I came across one of his posts. He was on a beach chair and was taking a picture of his two nephews playing in the water but had left his big old feet in the shot.

I don't know what made me reach out to him, but I probably felt a little guilty for leaving him hanging on that first text. Plus, I've already said he's an attractive man, and I was a little curious.

So I DMed him: "Nobody wants to see your feet."

That's right. That was my line. This is why I'm not writing a book on how to pick up men.

We ended up direct messaging for an hour. Finally, I shot my shot: "Bro, you got my number."

From there, we started talking all the time. We FaceTimed a lot too. By July, we were a couple. And I just *knew* Chad was the one.

Like I've said, I've dated men in the past who never wanted to share openly that they were with me. But that wasn't the case with Chad. He was open—proud, even—to be the guy on my arm. I've also dated men who kept their phones in their pockets at all times. You know the ones whose pants are vibrating during your entire date, and they don't take their phones out in front of you once? Not Chad. He'd have his phone sitting out on the table, face down and sound off, and I never *once* wondered who else he was communicating or engaging with.

I trusted him. He was faithful, committed, vulnerable, and transparent. Chad was everything I had ever whispered to God that I wanted.

Up until that point, I had kept myself in check.

But then the doubt started creeping in. The old patterns. Pretty soon, I was consumed again. Even after all that learning and all that practice and all that therapy. I let my thoughts pick me up and carry me through the next few months.

I started constructing reasons why Chad was eventually going to abandon me. It began as an, *I'm so lucky to be his,* and quickly devolved into, *Am I a good enough Christian to be his mate? Why did he choose me? An R&B singer? Why doesn't he go out and find a praise and worship leader? Or someone he can copastor with?*

My thoughts got downright crazy because I wasn't checking in with myself, God, good people—no one.

What if marrying me ruins his ministry? What if something from my past hinders what God wants to do in Chad's life and career? What if God has someone better for Chad, and he's just settling for me?

Chad tried to be patient with me, but I couldn't be reasoned with. I would pull away from him and put him on ice. Then I'd be needy and ask him why he was with me. He reassured me time and time again that I was the person he wanted to marry, but I still couldn't shake the feeling that no matter what Chad said, he didn't really want to spend the rest of his life with someone like me.

Now, I'm pretty sure the entire world knows what happened next (spoiler alert: huge, public breakdown). Since then, I've gone into the depths of hell psychologically and learned that I needed to get more real with myself and God than I had before.

I started praying. *God, show me what I'm not seeing in myself.*

*Teach me how to repair those parts of me that are still hurt and in need.
Help me accept your unconditional love and acceptance.*

During the course of my prayers and conversations with Sandy,
God kept bringing me back to the same scripture:

> May the God of hope fill you with all joy and peace in believing
> [through the experience of your faith] that by the power of the Holy
> Spirit you will abound in hope and overflow with confidence in His
> promises. (Romans 15:13)

I started thinking about that muddy cup of water I'd been carrying
around. The one with twigs and tiny little bugs and dirty rocks in it,
filled with the wounds I'd encountered over the years. I'd been offering
that cup to everyone I loved and expecting them to look at it as if it
were a crystal goblet of the finest wine.

I wondered how my life would be different if instead of my hurts
and disappointments, I offered others a glass full of joy. I wondered
what would happen if instead of walking around with a posture of
prove it, I walked around with a posture of *peace*. And I wondered how
things would change if instead of letting my past determine my value,
I embraced the hope of God with overflowing confidence.

I know some people roll their eyes when they're asked about their
childhood wounds. But for me, living through seven-year-old Michelle
and thirteen-year-old Michelle and even twenty-five-year-old Michelle
was no longer an option.

Maybe this is something you need to do in your own life. Maybe
you're repeating what you haven't repaired. I think in some ways, we
all are. And you may say, *Michelle, there's too much broken about my*

past to fix it. I get what it feels like to be overwhelmed. Just choose one situation with one person. Ask yourself the hard questions:

- *Why was I so sad or angry?*
- *What thoughts were behind the emotions?*
- *What beliefs were behind those thoughts?*

I had to revisit some painful moments. Out of respect for my parents and the journey of their lives together, I won't go further into detail. I had to deconstruct some beliefs in order to reconstruct new ones. I had to dump out my tall glass of pain so I could take my cup to God, ask him to clean it, and fill it up until it overflowed in confidence of his promises.

Chapter Five

I'VE GOT A CONFESSION TO MAKE. I LOVE TELEVISION.

Living alone does have its benefits, and one of those is that I watch what I want to watch when I want to watch it. There's no remote-control battle in my house. There's not even a remote control, because like a lot of you, I watch basically everything online.

I'd like to pause here to thank the good man/woman who invented streaming services. I honestly don't know what I'd do if I couldn't binge-watch *The First 48* at two o'clock in the morning when I can't sleep.

Yes, I watch shows about murder in the middle of the night so I can fall back to sleep. I don't judge you for being obsessed with pastry baking competitions, Janet, so let me live my life!

I love any show that involves crimes and investigations. I guess that's how I work out the criminal justice degree compulsion I never realized. But I'm so good at guessing who's guilty that I almost never make it to the end of an episode.

I've also been watching a lot of *American Greed* lately on CNBC. Can y'all believe there are still people swindling folks out of their money? It's crazy. People are still losing their retirements and savings accounts because somebody called them and said, "Yes, we'd like you to invest in so-and-so, and we can make you rich like *that* if you just hand over all your savings." Like, come on, y'all! If it's too good to be true, it's too good to be true.

Right now, I'm watching the Aaron Hernandez documentary on

Netflix. Y'all, it's just so interesting to me. How a man who obviously loved his daughter so much could be convicted of murder. How a dude with *so much success* could get so far off track. He seemed like a guy who was just torn between two identities. At the same time, I do think some folks on there are not being honest. They're a little too eager to get their screen time and share intimate details of a dead man's life. My lie radar is like, *Nah. You're just looking to get on television.* And I'm telling you, my lie radar is pretty dang accurate.

I'm not all dark and creepy, though. I watched the Kevin Hart series recently and laughed till I snorted. Kevin's a great guy, and he's so fun to watch. Of course I watched *The Masked Singer.* (A show I did in 2019—more on that later!) I didn't know who any of the other contestants on my season were; they did an awesome job keeping all that under wraps. I also like me some feel-good shows like *This Is Us* and *A Million Little Things.* Matter of fact, I usually end up with a fistful of snotty tissues by the time the credits run. They're tear-jerkers, but I love the writing and the beautiful relationships they've created. It hurts so good!

I could spend a month in bed watching all the movies nominated for awards shows. But most of them wind up depressing or frustrating me, so I'm trying not to do that. Like, why would I spend three hours cheering for someone's story just to get to the end and they die? Or worse, get to the end and there is no end! It's all artsy and ambiguous. Maybe my movie aesthetic isn't developed to their level, but I'm like, *Wait, that's not the credits rolling, right? We still don't know why this, this, and this happened! We still don't know if she ever finds out the truth! We. Still. Don't. Know!* Nothing irks me like an unsatisfying ending. A bad ending is better than no ending.

Maybe that's why I'm such a big Judge Judy fan. No, I really am. If I'm anywhere in the world where there's cable, I always turn on the TV's guide channel and look for Judge Judy. And Judge Judy, my friends, never has an ambiguous ending. Nope. That gavel gets tapped every single time.

I love Judge Judy because she tells it like it is. I admire her ability to just cut through the bull and be direct with people. I consider myself a blunt person, but I got nothing on Judge Judith Sheindlin. When you leave her courtroom, you know exactly where you stand. I mean, she will probably call you an idiot along the way, but that's usually because you're being an idiot.

And if I've learned one thing from watching Judge Judy, it's this: be careful what you come to agreement on.

One of my favorite episodes has the single quickest judgment handed down that I've ever seen. Okay, here's the backstory. The plaintiff in the case—a high school–aged girl, mind you—claimed that the defendant, a grown man, stole some valuables from her, including her wallet with about fifty dollars in it, a calculator, and an earpiece.

Right in the middle of her explanation, the defendant had the nerve to interrupt. He said, "There was no earpiece, ma'am."

I was like, *Run that back. He did not just say that.*

I couldn't believe what I'd just heard. That dumb dang thief admitted he'd stolen the rest of the stuff. He accidentally came into agreement with the plaintiff by correcting her statement. Because how are you going to know what is and isn't in a woman's bag if you didn't go through and take her stuff?

Judge Judy started laughing. "Decision in favor of the plaintiff."

The whole thing lasted twenty-six seconds.

I'm being serious when I tell you this—I stopped and thought for a minute. How many times had I agreed to something by accident?

You know what I mean. Like the one time I told my girlfriend Jodi I'd pet sit for her while she went to Hawaii with her mom and sister. In my mind, that meant I'd stop by her condo once a day and pour a can of dog food in the bowl for her Yorkie, Charlie. Charlie eats once a day and uses these little miracle puppy pads to potty. He doesn't even have to go outside! All I had to do was feed Charlie, then throw away his used tinkle pads and put out new ones.

But I had no idea what I'd actually agreed to.

On the very first day, Charlie wouldn't eat. He just wouldn't do it. I tried everything. I cleaned the food bowl, I mopped the floor around it, I went to the store and bought identical food and tried that. Nope. He'd walk to the bowl, sniff it, and sit down and look at me like, "What else ya got?"

I don't even have to tell you that I was sweating by the third day when he still refused his food. I googled the living heck out of every search I could think of that might help, but they all led me to the conclusion that either Charlie wasn't hungry or he was about to drop dead of stomach cancer.

So I'm praying over a dog like he's my spouse on his death bed. Charlie wasn't dying on my watch.

Then I went back to Google: *emotional reasons dogs won't eat.* Now I'm a dog therapist. I tried to psychoanalyze the situation. Sometimes dogs won't eat if they feel anxious or stressed. Wasn't nobody in that condo more anxious or stressed than I was, but I thought if Charlie knew I was Jodi's homie, he'd eat a little. Would y'all believe that at one point, I played a video of Jodi and me together and showed it to Charlie to help him trust me?

But Charlie, God bless his stubborn doggy soul, he stood his ground. We were in an all-out standoff. Me and this white ball of fluff with huge brown eyes—brown eyes that were judging your girl like, *This ain't how Mama makes my lunch.* So, I broke down and texted Jodi. I felt legitimate shame, bothering her on her girls' trip because I couldn't get a three-pound dog to take a bite of food.

"Oh, Charlie does this sometimes when his stomach is upset. There's some boiled chicken in the fridge. Just warm some of that up."

So now I'm cooking for Charlie. First time, I think I got the chicken too hot. He wouldn't even get close to the bowl. I threw that out. Second time, I got out a cooking thermometer and googled the temperature to serve a dog boiled chicken and got that bowl *just right.*

I about shouted hallelujah when Charlie took that first bite. It was kind of like he didn't even want to give in to me, but he was too hungry to put up a fight. I gave myself a little pat on the back and went home.

The next day I came in, and before I even got through the door, I knew something was wrong. I *smelled* something was wrong.

Dog. Poop. Everywhere. I didn't know it was possible for a dog that small to contain so much poop, but there it was. All over Jodi's bed— the pillows, the comforter, the sheets. Somehow he even managed to get the bed skirt. Apparently, eating a full bowl of boiled chicken after a three-day food stalemate had an adverse effect on Charlie's bowels.

So now I'm cleaning for Charlie. I didn't have the stomach for the situation, so I took that stuff to the cleaners for same-day service. When I brought it all back, I was afraid to leave Charlie alone for the night, so I slept on Jodi's sofa. *Sleep* is a term I use loosely here, since I mostly just laid awake, waiting on him to explode again.

The rest of the week went by without much more action, but I was exhausted. I had agreed to do one thing but had unintentionally agreed to a whoooole lot of other things too. I had agreed to be a chef, a therapist, a veterinarian, a personal assistant, a housekeeper, *and* a pet sitter.

Be careful what you agree to, folks. Just be careful.

I mean, this isn't news to y'all. You know this. You're all probably really responsible people who read the fine print before signing the cell-phone agreement, right? Okay, that's an extreme example—ain't nobody got time for that. Apple's probably got us all pledging our undying loyalty until the end of time, and none of us even know it.

What I'm really talking about is, are we careful about agreeing to things that *really* matter? When it matters to our lives? To our bodies? To our hearts? And by agreeing, I mean repeating things—either in our thoughts or with our words—to ourselves or others.

Did you know that if a person talks out loud to a plant consistently, it will grow faster? Look, I didn't believe it when I first heard it either. But it's true! Matter of fact, one study showed that plants not only grow better when talked to regularly, but that a woman's voice makes a plant grow faster than a man's.[1] Okay, now ladies! Talk about girl power.

Your voice—your inner voice too—gives life to whatever you give it to.

If you're a believer, you've probably heard the scripture from Proverbs 18:21 that says, "Your tongue has the power of life and death. Those who love to talk will eat the fruit of their words" (NIRV).

If you don't think that what you say to yourself or to others has any bearing on your life, you are in danger. Our words and agreements work like magnets that draw us in a certain direction. Even if it's a direction we don't want to go in.

Think about it this way: If you wake up every day and say, "It's going to be an awful day," everything you do and say that day will be done and said through that negative lens. You're going to look for the bad, and every time you see it, you'll say, "See, I was right. It's an awful day."

I've seen this in my own life. When Chad and I got engaged, it wasn't long before I began to say, "We'll never make it down the aisle." I said it over and over and over again to myself. Probably even to some other people too. I would read comments online saying Chad and I were doomed, and you know what? I came into agreement with those statements. I agreed so often that I started having dreams about it.

One dream I'd have was at the venue on the day of our wedding. All the guests were arriving, the cake was set out, the flowers were everywhere. Everything was beautiful. So. It was time for me to get in my dress, and I looked at my sister and said, "I don't have my dress. I can't get married." And that was that. For whatever reason, my not having a dress meant things were over for Chad and me.

Another dream I had was similar. Everyone was at the venue on the big day, and I knew they were all waiting for me to come down the aisle. I was wearing a bodice, like the top of a wedding dress. I had a bunch of skirts to choose from, but I couldn't decide. I looked to my friend and said, "Tell Chad to wait on me." But he wouldn't. Again, my wardrobe issues meant Chad and I weren't going to get married.

And you may say, "Michelle, lots of people have anxious dreams before they get married," but these were different. Since I had already made an agreement in my spirit that Chad and I would never make it down the aisle, these dreams served as *confirmation* to me that the wedding would never happen.

Instead of waking up and saying, "Dang, I got some issues when it comes to getting ready for marriage. What is it that's making me have these dreams?" I woke up and said, "See! I knew it. I knew he'd leave me/I'd screw it up/something would happen. I knew we'd never get married, and that dream just confirms what I already know."

Now, had I been checking in with myself and being honest with myself, I would have taken these thoughts captive and said, "Okay, what's really going on here?" But I wasn't being honest with myself. To me, agreeing that my relationship would fail was my way of protecting myself. It was my way of rejecting Chad before he rejected me. It was my way of guarding my heart in case the engagement was broken.

And guess what. The engagement was broken. (More on that later.)

But we do this all the time, whether we realize it or not. Don't think so?

Do you ever find yourself saying yes when you really want to say no? We all do this occasionally, but how many of you continually find yourself going places and doing things you really don't want to do? Do you put your wants and needs on the back burner and put other people's (or even animals') needs first, even when it's a real inconvenience to you? Is doing something for someone else the only way you feel good about yourself? Making someone else happy? Even if it makes you unhappy?

If this is you, you may have made a spiritual agreement a while back that on your own, you're no good. That without works, you are worthless. You've told yourself that everybody relies on you and you can't let them down. If you do, you're selfish. So you find yourself enslaved to the demands of those around you. You're probably frustrated, drained, and feel taken advantage of. But it's all because you haven't checked in with your motives, your *why* behind the choices you make.

How about this one. Are you someone who is constantly anxious, nervous, or worried? Do you walk around holding your breath, waiting for the other shoe to drop? When one of your worries or fears disappears or becomes resolved, do you immediately replace it with another?

Do you tend to overanalyze conversations and interactions to the point where you're breaking down someone's tone of voice and body language regularly?

Your boss suggested you go on break five minutes early, and your anxiety writes an entire story that ends in you being fired or quitting for no reason. You're like, *Now, when the boss said take your lunch break five minutes early, did he emphasize the word* early? *Did he raise his eyebrow at the end of that sentence? Does that mean he saw me checking Instagram and wanted me off the clock? Wasn't he on the phone after that? Did he call his supervisor? I think I saw them talking before I left. I bet they were talking about me. I bet they want to fire me.*

If this is you, maybe you've agreed that you don't deserve good things. You don't deserve happiness, peace, or joy like everyone else. So you're constantly waiting for something bad to happen.

Part of checking in with yourself is becoming aware of what thoughts you're having over and over again. These are usually signs of agreements you've made about yourself internally: spiritually, mentally, and emotionally.

Part of checking in with yourself is becoming aware of what thoughts you're having over and over again.

The Bible puts it this way:

> The weapons of our warfare are not physical [weapons of flesh and
> blood]. Our weapons are divinely powerful for the destruction of
> fortresses. We are destroying sophisticated arguments and every
> exalted and proud thing that sets itself up against the [true] knowl-
> edge of God, and we are taking every thought and purpose captive
> to the obedience of Christ. (2 Corinthians 10:4–5)

Our minds, our thoughts, and the things we come into agreement
on matter so much because they all work together to pull and push our
lives in certain directions. The stakes are too high to call this thing
a struggle or fight. In other words, this is war! We are "destroying"
arguments by bringing every thought we have, especially thoughts
we repeat over and over again, before God. If it doesn't line up with
something he's said or reflect the love and value he has for us, then we
should cast those ideas as far away from us as we can!

We shouldn't invite negative thoughts over for dinner, move them
in, and share a bed with them. But that's so often what we (including
me) end up doing.

For me, morning time is when I'm the most anxious. It's like I
wake up to the Enemy standing at my bedside with a tray of my mistakes for breakfast. And you know he's got some orange juice with him,
because he knows I've got a lot of regret to swallow. That's when I have
to work hard to check in with myself and recognize, *Okay, Michelle.
You're thinking some weird things right now.*

I've got a spoiler alert for you: there is no nicely-tied-bow-ending
to this book. While I have come so far in the checking-in process, I am

still human. I have bad days. I have bad weeks, even. I'm in this thing *with* you, not in front of you.

That being said, this week has been tough. For one, I'm currently living in Atlanta, and the weather here this week has been depressing. It's been rainy, foggy, and dark all day. And a sweet friend of mine just lost her husband and child in an accident, and I am right in the thick of that mental warfare the Bible tells us about.

I like waking up to sunshine pouring in and birds singing and a cloudless sky. When it's moody outside, it's moody inside too. I've had zero motivation to leave my place, and the isolation is not good for me. I wake up and there's no sun. There are no birds. The only sound I hear is the rain slapping against my windows. The bed is made up on one side, and there's only one nightstand being used.

There was a time I used to wake up and look at my phone, knowing there'd be a sweet text waiting for me. Now I reach for it and think, *Those days are gone forever. This is your life, Michelle. You won't ever have that again.*

Now, what? Why would I even say that? Why would I even think that? If I were that desperate for a man to text me in the morning, I'd go and find one. But that's not it. I don't want just any man, I want *the one.* And God is still working on me. He's not done with me yet. It's not a matter of *if* God will keep his promises to me, but *when.* It's not that it's never going to happen, it's that it hasn't happened *yet.*

When I'm feeling good and checking in with myself, when I'm taking my thoughts captive, I can do that. I can stop these extreme thoughts of *It's never going to happen for me* and reason with them. But on weeks like this one, it's easy to slip into that same old negative rotation of thoughts.

So I have to start each and every day with prayer. I'm not saying that's what everybody has to do, but it's what I have to do. Because I don't want to go into my day with any wrong agreements that are going to move me in a wrong direction. I ask God to remind me to check in. I ask him to put a check on my spirit when I'm about to agree to something that is not his will for me.

Then, throughout the day, when I'm doing what I need to be doing, I check in with my thoughts.

Figure out a system that you can stick to. Whether it's a thought-by-thought thing or whether you pause at certain times of the day to think through the things you're repeating to yourself.

If my thought pattern doesn't line up with the Word of God or the character of God, I will literally say, sometimes out loud, "I do not agree with that."

That ain't right!

Nope.

Not today, Satan.

Not tomorrow either.

Chapter Six

OVER THE YEARS I'VE DONE HUNDREDS AND HUNDREDS of interviews with the media. Do you want to know which question pops up in a shocking number of those?

"Michelle, tell us about your most embarrassing moment."

And that makes sense, right? It's a question that helps people relate to you. Like, *See! Michelle's just like you! She drops ketchup on every daggum white thing she wears!* (Which is accurate.) Only in my case, y'all already know the answer because you've seen it. The entire *world* has seen it.

No one will ever let me live down the time I fell flat on my face on live TV while filming a spot on BET. (Pauses for all y'all to google this fall and refresh your memories.)

You know how some people tell an embarrassing story and say, "There were like a million people watching!" Well, there were literally a million people watching. Actually, millions. I was performing with Destiny's Child to promote our last album, *Destiny Fulfilled*, on BET's *106 and Park*. If you've ever seen MTV's *Total Recall Live* (*TRL*), *106 and Park* is basically identical to it. So there we were, in our fierce-looking outfits, and we were about to sing "Soldier" on live television.

Our intro was cute. We were just supposed to strut down the middle of the stage and then hit a couple dance moves once we started singing. Only, I took about one or two steps before my heel got caught in the decorative loops on the bottom of my pants.

One minute I was strutting, and the next I was literally face-down on the floor. In my head, I was like, *Okay, these are professional camera operators. Surely they panned to the audience or cut to another angle. I'm fine. Everything's fine.* So I hopped back up and got back to dancing.

Only thing is, they were shooting with one camera. Nothing to pan to. Nothing but me and my abundance of grace.

Might I remind you that this was live TV. Live, live, live, no-delay *live* television. And Destiny's Child was *known* for being on point. We were more than on point—we were *the* point. We were known for our perfect performances. From our coordinating wardrobe, to our fabulous hair, to our shimmering makeup, and especially when it came to our intricate choreography. Then, there I am, flopping to the ground like a fish out of water, and I'm not even doing a complicated move. Not even walking down steps. Not doing anything more difficult than walking. We weren't even singing yet!

By the time we finished our song and got backstage, the memes were already being created. Thanks to YouTube and the rest of social media, that trip became the Fall Seen Around the World. To this day, more than fifteen years later, I am still tagged in something at least once a week related to that fall. I mean, I guess I should actually thank the little internet wizards who make all this stuff, because y'all are making your girl relevant every time it gets reposted.

Note to any performers out there: I remember hearing once that Michael Jackson always rehearsed in the clothes he was going to perform in or something identical. And the man never missed a beat. He definitely never fell during a live taping on BET in front of millions of viewers.

Always rehearse in what you're gonna perform in! This was one of the few times we didn't. But you best believe we did every single time after that.

By that time I'd been in Destiny's Child for years. I was hyper-aware of the fact that I wasn't the star. For a lot of folks, it was Beyoncé, Kelly, and "that other girl."

Take *Saturday Night Live*, for example. Poking fun at me gave them plenty of material for episodes. I guess having your job performance satirized by some of the funniest people on the planet is a sideways compliment; but most days it feels really, really sideways. Now let's talk about fan sites. Want to know my most famous fan site? PoorMichelle.com. What I will say about that site is that I wish they'd have consulted with my accountant, because honestly, they've got their facts wrong.

Okay, clapbacks aside, you'd have to be cold, dead, and in the grave for others' perception of you to have no effect on your self-esteem. Especially when that perception is shared and perpetuated by the media.

Look, I knew I wasn't the girl boys were buying posters of and hanging on their walls. I knew I wasn't a sex symbol. I knew I had a reputation as the "church girl." And I also knew that sex sells.

Like I've said, I grew up with the message that I'm not worth sticking around for, that I'm not valuable or meaningful enough on my own. So, yeah. All this talk and chatter and media coverage irritated those wounds. Sometimes I think people assume celebrities are like robots. Like we just go look at our money and automatically feel better. But that is ridiculous. I'm a human just like you're a human. The same stuff that bothers you, frustrates you, and hurts you does all that to me.

Except I had paparazzi in my face asking me how it felt to be the punchline to a joke every time I went out.

So, yeah. I dealt with an enormous amount of anxiety.

Maybe they're right. Maybe I should quit. Maybe I'm not talented. Maybe I am a joke. Maybe I am _____ (fill in the blank). Every bad thing that was said about me has echoed in my heart as truth at some point or another.

But there's a big ole problem with that. Anxiety is not a representation of truth. Anxiety is a representation of what we fear.

Let me say that again.

Anxiety has no relationship with truth. Anxiety is nothing more than our fears magnified.

Here's my anxious thought: *Everyone thinks I'm a joke. Everyone thinks I'm a terrible singer and didn't belong in Destiny's Child.*

Here's what's true: My voice isn't the biggest or most commercial voice that's ever carried a tune. But I am a talented singer, songwriter, and performer. I've sold millions of records. I have a successful career that many people grow up dreaming about. What's true is that I know I'm not everybody's favorite Destiny's Child member, but do you know what else is true? Honey, I still. Got. Paid.

See, the tricky thing about anxiety is that we sometimes think we're feeling anxious about something because it's rooted in fact. Like, *this* could *happen because I've seen this happen in other people's lives.* Or, *I've seen this happen in my own life before.* So there's "truth" to the anxiety I'm feeling.

But if you were to bring that thought before God and say, "God, how much of this is truth and how much of this is fear?" and you really broke down your anxiety thought by thought, like

Anxiety
is not a
representation
of truth.
Anxiety is a
representation
of what
we fear.

I just did, you'd see that you're not fearing the truth. You're fearing your fear.

Now, that's not to say we shouldn't check in with these thoughts and ask, "Is there any truth to this?" Because we should. I'm not saying we should live in denial. What I am saying is we have to check in with our thoughts and throw out the fear and work with the facts.

Because sometimes, we can have *intuition*.

In my opinion, the Holy Spirit cautions us when we're about to tread somewhere we don't need to. You may not be comfortable thinking about the Holy Spirit, and that's okay. Basically, when you enter into a relationship with Jesus, his Holy Spirit has access to lead you, guide you, comfort you, and speak to you. When I have intuitions, I believe they are given to me by the Holy Spirit.

Let me give you a few examples.

When I last left off with my story about Chad and me, we were getting serious.

On March 21, 2018, in Pebble Beach, California, at a beautiful resort, Chad asked me to be his wife. He actually did a really good job with all of it; even with all my sleuthing skills, I had no idea he was going to propose.

Chad and his best friend, Shawn, were part of an organization that held a charity golf tournament the weekend of our one-year anniversary. Before I could get mad about Chad playing golf on our big day, weeks before the event Chad had told me about the tournament and invited me to come. He sold the idea by saying that he would get a room for me, that we'd get to eat all our meals at yummy places, and that I could get all these fancy spa treatments while I was there.

Say no more, Chad. I'm in.

I had been looking forward to that weekend since he'd told me about it. Getting massages, hanging out at fire pits, eating good food, doing girly stuff with girlfriends while the boys swing their clubs? That's heaven to me. And if you're sporty, that's amazing. I work out, and I work out hard and love it. But when it comes to golf? I don't know how to golf. I don't know if I have the patience for golf. But what I do have the patience for is a nice seventy-five-minute body scrub.

The morning of the proposal, I think that's when I got a body scrub. Because mind you, every day I was getting treatments, and they all ran together in the most delicious way, but I think that day was the day of my body scrub. Honestly, I had no idea that I was getting scrubbed up to have my body polished and shined for this proposal.

After the scrub it was around noon, and we got dressed to meet the boys for lunch. Now, you know how this is—you're on vacation with your man, so you're adding a little something extra to the ensemble. You're curling that hair a little tighter and putting on mascara after not wearing it for weeks. But the boys were late.

I was getting so mad because I was like, *Where are Chad and Shawn? Don't they know I've worked up an appetite today getting this body scrubbed and enjoying fire pits? What are they doing that's more important than feeding me?*

Isn't that how every girl is the day she gets engaged? Annoyed at some point and then low-key embarrassed after she figures it all out. Well, that was definitely me.

Eventually they got there, and we went to eat.

So we got to lunch, and we were just sitting around talking, and Chad would just look at me and smile. I thought he felt bad for making me starve, or that maybe I was looking extra scrubbed and fine, so I didn't think much of it. Everything was normal until the server came up and handed me an iPad.

I was like, *Oh, this is a high-tech restaurant. The lunch menu is on an iPad! We fancy now. That's amazing. So convenient. The servers don't have to write down our order or try to memorize it. I can just tap whatever I want, and then the chef gets it and they prepare the meal.*

Right, Michelle. Right. I'm sure everybody around me knew what was going on. Everybody but me.

Then Chad told me to press play, so I did. And a video started. I was like, "What is this? What's going on?" still not understanding why the restaurant's menu iPad had a video I needed to see.

But no one at the table answered me. And that's when the mood really shifted.

On the screen, I saw Chad at an airport. He looked at the camera and said, "Come on, take this journey with me."

Then he got on a plane and was flying through the night. The next shot was Chad hanging out with my two cousins at a restaurant, eating together. They were just joking and laughing, making cracks about who was going to pay the bill. In the background was one of my favorite songs, "Living for the Love of You" by the Isley Brothers.

I had no idea when this had been taped, but seeing them together hit me hard. My cousins are like brothers to me, and it's always been my dream for my husband and my family to get along and love spending time together. I think that's what marriage should be: two entire families joining together as one. Two families joining together in purpose, prayer, life, all of it together.

Then my uncle came on the screen. He's a physician and a pastor, and he was all dressed in his scrubs. He and Chad were sitting and talking. At one point, my uncle put his stethoscope up to Chad's heart to listen to it, and they were laughing and cutting up. Then they prayed together.

My uncle is like a second father to me. So, at that point, you know I started just boo-hooing. No, I'll be honest with y'all, it was probably more like wailing.

And the whole time I was watching this at the restaurant, I was literally like, "What in the world is this?" It wasn't until Chad actually started proposing that I had any idea what he'd done, what the video meant.

Chad had flown to my hometown of Rockford, Illinois, and he had basically asked my entire family for my hand in marriage. Not just my parents. He took the time and made the effort to ask everyone, even extended family. He met, like, six or seven of my mom's brothers and sisters over at my aunt Jackie's house. She's the matriarch of the family, by the way. So after you go through my mom, you have to go through her sister Jackie to marry me.

At the end of the video, another one of my favorite songs started playing, "Take the World" by Johnnyswim. My family had thrown Chad a surprise party before he left, and the shots flashed from Chad with my niece, to Chad with my aunts, to Chad with my dad. Then Chad prayed with my entire family. This video is to this day seriously one of the most beautiful things I've ever seen.

I was losing it by that point. I was screaming. I kept saying I was going to stop crying, but I didn't. Shawn and his wife, Leslie, were crying. Chad was crying. We were all a mess.

The very last shot was of Chad recreating the first text he ever sent me. You know, the one where he asked if I wanted to "connect." (Insert eye roll. Chad! C'mon, bro.) He "sent" the text again, only he added, *Forever this time.*

Okay, by now your girl had *finally* caught on. I looked up from the video, and Chad was getting on one knee. He said so many beautiful things. So many wonderful, meaningful things that I'll hide in my heart forever.

Now, Chad had been saving up money for *ten years* to buy his future wife a ring. And when he popped open that box, I about shouted hallelujah. I was almost hysterical, I was so giddy. He did good—real, real good. But to be honest, I would have taken a plastic vending machine ring from that man.

Looking back, I hate that what we've gone through sort of tarnishes the effort that he put into proposing to me. It is probably the most wonderful thing any human has ever done for me.

Our love was real and it was big. But in the end, I would let my anxiety become bigger. I would let the false feelings become so big that they would devour everything that was real, what my intuition told me was true.

Even as early as the minute Chad started proposing, I let doubt creep in. The whole time he was on his knee, I was thinking, *I've still got a lot of work to do on myself. I'm not where I want to be as a woman. I'm not qualified to be someone's wife yet.*

And yet this guy got on one knee, and he proposed to me. He told me his life was better because I was in it. He said he never wanted to live his life without me.

Intuition would say, *Michelle, this man seeks God. This man has prayed about this. You have prayed about this. God has you right where you're supposed to be.*

Those thoughts reflect the facts.

Michelle, you're not good enough to be married to a pastor. You need to know more Scripture. You need to get more experience in ministry. You need to get more distance from your R&B past.

Those thoughts reflected my feelings.

Which one of those do you think I checked in with? Want to guess?

Y'all already know.

Immediately, I relied on my feelings (anxiety) and not the facts (intuition) to direct my path moving forward.

Not long after we were engaged, Chad and I started filming a reality show. We had been told by so many people that we should do a show, that social media loved Chad and me together, that the world needed to see a celebrity couple who loved God on TV. So I got counsel and advice from someone in the industry. They started helping Chad and me formulate a pitch and helped us sort out what our "angle" would be.

Offers started coming in, and it was crazy. I was like, *People really care what Chad and I talk about at dinner?* But it was more than that for us. Chad and I genuinely wanted to be an example of two broken people who loved Jesus and were trying to make love work.

We were sorting through which network to go with when the Oprah Winfrey Network came in at the last minute. It wasn't even a discussion after that. OWN would produce our show.

The premise of *Chad Loves Michelle* was to follow our journey to the altar and to focus on our experience in marriage counseling.

People were also very interested in our story because we were abstaining from sex—something our culture finds incredibly shocking. Because of that, and the fact that so many people close to us had never done marriage counseling, we were all about it. So we were like, "Well, why don't we just set up the cameras in our actual therapy sessions?" And that's really as organic and raw as it should have been.

But by the time everything was signed and it got to the hands of producers, we got awful news. We couldn't film our marriage counseling because of a licensing agreement with the curriculum we were going through. We were studying out of a book called *Before You Say I Do* by H. Norman Wright and Wes Roberts. It was so good. And we *so* wanted to show people our hearts about dating, about marriage, about abstinence, about trying to follow God's will through the engagement process.

But that's not what ended up happening.

I truly, truly regret doing that show. If I had to rank all my career moves in order, doing that show would be dead last.

But before the show, my intuition told me not to do it. I just didn't listen.

I will never forget Chad and me driving down the highway one day before we agreed to do the show. We were talking about whether or not we should commit to it, and out of nowhere I just said, "I don't feel *right* about it. It doesn't sit well with me."

That should have been a red flag. Like, flaming-on-fire-call-911 red flag. Any time we get that little uncomfortable feeling, that tickle in our conscience, that whisper in our spirits, we should stop what we're doing and check in with it. Bring it to God. Don't just say, "God, give me a sign!" Even though I don't think there's anything necessarily wrong with that, he's already given you one. Your intuition is telling you, *Pause. Take caution. Slow down.*

Anytime you want to know what the Holy Spirit is trying to tell you, line up your feelings with his Word. Or, like I do, take a couple of minutes to journal about it. I type in my phone's notepad. If I'd have done that, if I'd have checked in with that intuitive part of my mind and soul that was whispering no, I bet I would have gotten confirmation that it wasn't wise for Chad and me to do the show.

See, sometimes a thing isn't a "good" choice or a "bad" choice; sometimes a thing is just an unwise choice.

But then another side of me thought, *You're going to be nervous doing anything for the first time. You've never done this before. It's just nerves.* I thought, *The world needs to see Chad and me striving for celibacy. They need to see the ups and downs of a relationship and how to rely on God during both.* I was so sure that Chad and I wouldn't succumb to the reality TV show curse. Maybe there was a part of me that wanted to prove we were different from other couples. That our way of doing things was the "right" way.

Some of these thoughts were guilt driven. Is guilt of God? Nope.

Some of these thoughts were pride driven. What does God say about pride? It comes right before a fall.

Some of these thoughts were just plain stupid. If I'd have run them through the filter of common sense, I would never have agreed to the show.

But I'd get this intuitive feeling that something wasn't right about doing it, and before I even checked in with it, I'd dismiss it. I'd say, "You're just scared," and keep on doing what I wanted. If I'd have just slowed down, if I'd have taken the time to pray, journal, and seek the advice of more people, I probably would have realized what was fact:

Fact 1: I knew I really did have a lot of growing to do outside of my relationship with Chad. I should have been preparing myself *privately* to be his wife.

Fact 2: While it is my responsibility to show others God's goodness, it's not my responsibility to put on a marriage clinic before I've even been married. Chad and I had no business trying to teach folks how to be engaged when we had only been engaged for ten minutes.

Fact 3: The media is unpredictable. I've seen it tear apart the strongest, most God-fearing people in the industry. What made me think that Chad and I would be different? Pride. Honey, pride ain't done a good thing for anyone in a relationship. Self-respect, yes. But pride? No way.

Fact 4: How honestly could a person really live their lives with a camera following them around? I don't care who you are, when the cameras are on, you're aware of it. And even if that fact only changes one or two reactions or conversations, those could be pivotal moments of vulnerability lost forever.

If I had listened to my intuition, if I had checked in with that *knowing* feeling and chosen fact over feeling . . . at the very least, it would have saved me, Chad, and a bunch of our loved ones a whole lot of hurt, embarrassment, and anger.

Why is it that we'll get married to anxiety but we tell our intuition to shut its mouth and go to bed without supper? For one, it's hard to know the difference until you're on the wrong side of an unwise choice. It's easy to look back and say, "I wish I'd slowed down. I wish I'd thought about that a little longer." This is especially true if you've dealt with any kind of real anxiety. When people tell you to "trust your gut," you want to be like, "Cool, well yesterday my gut told me it was a good idea to call in sick to work, eat ice cream straight out the tub, and not leave my house all day."

Our anxiety has robbed many of us of the ability to check in with that inner voice—the voice of the Holy Spirit, the voice of God.

So let's break it down. How do you know the difference?

One test is to ask, "Am I just *scared*? Or is it something more?"

Like, if you're afraid of flying and you're waiting to board the plane and all of a sudden your heart starts racing, your palms are sweaty, and you can't catch your breath. Your anxiety will try to trick you into thinking that's intuition, that it's a sign your plane is going to explode in midair.

But all those thoughts are based in fear and not in fact. That's not your intuition talking; that's your crazy.

One of the biggest differences between anxiety and intuition is the way they make you feel. Since intuition is from God, it should leave you feeling a little more relaxed, a little more at peace. But anxiety? Anxiety is not of God. I personally think anxiety is from the pit of hell. And it comes on you like a cold grip around your heart, making you feel nauseous, panicky, and unsure.

Take me riding in the car with Chad, for example. The words "I don't feel right about this" just fell out of my mouth. I hadn't even realized I was thinking that. And when I said it, I had none of the symptoms that my usual anxiety brings: racing pulse, manic thoughts, a sense of overwhelming dread and doom. Actually, I felt better after saying those words out loud.

Listen to the way Proverbs 2:6–10 explains intuition from God:

> For the LORD gives [skillful and godly] wisdom;
> From His mouth come knowledge and understanding.
> He stores away sound wisdom for the righteous [those who are in
> right standing with Him];
> He is a shield to those who walk in integrity [those of honorable
> character and moral courage],
> He guards the paths of justice;
> And He preserves the way of His saints (believers).
> Then you will understand righteousness and justice [in every
> circumstance]
> And integrity and every good path.
> For [skillful and godly] wisdom will enter your heart
> And knowledge will be pleasant to your soul.

Anxiety is unsettling. It feels like an anchor dragging our very being into a pit of dark despair. But intuition? Intuition will feel "pleasant" to your soul. Not great, but pleasant. Intuition ain't gonna make you jump for joy. But it will feel quietly true, and truth brings out peace and rest.

Not checking in with that still, quiet voice in my spirit cost me a great deal. I traded Chad's words for anxiety. I traded God's words for anxiety. I traded what I *knew* to be fact for fiction.

And I had no idea what I would lose before it was all said and done.

Chapter Seven

I WENT PUBLIC WITH MY DEPRESSION BY ACCIDENT.

In 2013 I was doing a round of media for a Broadway musical that I was touring in called *Fela!* There I was, doing an interview with someone from the Associated Press about the show, and the interview just started feeling like a conversation. (Sign of a good interviewer!) And before you know it, I was talking about how the prior year had been a very difficult one for me because I had struggled with depression.

Once I said it, I was like, *Oh my gosh, what did I just say?* But once I had released those words into the universe, there was no catching them and shoving them back in. And while it was a very respectful interview, it went everywhere. I mean, it was on the ticker tape of CNN. And I was like, *Lord have mercy, what did I just do? What did* you *just do?*

Not long after that, I did *Good Morning America* for that same round of media. I remember a man, an older man, pulled me to the side with tears in his eyes right there in the studio. And he just thanked me profusely. He thanked me for talking about my depression publicly, for giving the world a point of reference for all those who suffer in silence.

I didn't go into any personal details with him, and I didn't want him to feel like he had to divulge anything personal to me. But I just encouraged him to get help, and I told him that he wasn't alone. I think we all need to hear that we're not the only ones. Especially men suffering from depression. They're not as open to discussing something so tender and so fragile and so vulnerable. It's not "manly" to be depressed.

The topic came up again when I was on *The Talk* in 2017. In that interview, I actually went further to say that I had experienced suicidal thoughts. Again, I hadn't planned on saying that, but I did. My words were like tiny rubber balls that pinged off that stage into the laps of every major news outlet in the country. And again, I was like, *Good gracious, Michelle. Get ahold of your mouth, child!*

But you know what? Once again, I experienced this incredible response of, "Thank you. You showed me I'm not the only one. You taught me I can overcome this. You inspired me to talk to someone about how I'm feeling." The more I've shared, the more people in my life and around me have been able to share too.

One thing I think I'd want anyone suffering from depression to hear is that depression is not who you are. It's certainly not who I am. There is *so* much more to you than what you're feeling. And there is so much more to me.

In fact, when I sat down to write this book, I thought, *What else do I want people to know about me?* Because I'm obviously not trying to tell y'all that I've got this all figured out. I'm not trying to say, "Do what I did." No, in some cases it's "Do the opposite of what I did." I just want to share my heart with you. I want to share my story. And I hope that along the way you get to know me—the real me.

First, I want you to know that I love God with everything. Like, my love for him is so deep and real. And that's not props to me at all. I have grown in my relationship with God because of all he's brought me through. You know if all God did was send Jesus to die for me, that would have been enough? But every day he shows up somehow, some way. The least I can do is show up every day with him too. I'd say my love for God is the most important thing about me.

Other than that, I've got to be honest with y'all. I'm pretty boring. Over the last few years, I've turned into an introvert. Though I love people, I have no problem being comfortable by myself.

I'm probably a lot like you. I have fears and concerns like you do. I compare prices; I don't like overpaying for stuff. I jam out in my car and get caught by people driving next to me. I run my own social media. Anything you see posted to my Instagram or Twitter, it's me posting it.

Oh, and I love to laugh. I'm a goofball. I love to crack jokes. My filter for those jokes is getting looser and looser these days. People always meet me and think I'm so serious. But after five minutes, they're like, *Okay, okay. There's a little personality in there!* Oh, and I love cars. I love driving. I love road trips. I can do five hours straight and not stop if I don't have to.

Aside from my love for God, the next thing I think it's important for you to know is that I am human. I am *deeply* human, if you know what I'm saying! I am complex. I am imperfect. And I've got a temper. I've got a mouth on me, baaaby. And that mouth has gotten me into some trouble.

Which brings me back to my relationship with Chad.

When Chad and I got engaged, I was actually in the middle of rehearsals for Coachella. Matter of fact, when I got engaged, the first people I called after my mama were Beyoncé and Kelly. Then I called my friend Amy down in Miami, but that was supposed to be it. Because of course, Chad and I had signed on for our reality show, and we were supposed to keep our engagement under wraps so the episode could be the big reveal. So from jump, it was like there was this sense of *Is this real?* when I thought about Chad and me getting married.

After our weekend at the golf tournament, I went right back to rehearsals, trying my best not to tell every stranger on the street our news, which was harder than I thought it'd be. I'm normally a very private person. There were rumors for the longest time that I didn't date men because I never posted about it or talked about it. But this was different for me.

Chad and I were so excited. I mean, we were like little kids on Christmas morning. We wanted to tell everybody. We had found love and found each other, and we wanted the world to know. So I may have kept my mouth shut for the most part, but I practically walked around with my left hand up in front of my face like, *Notice anything different about that ring finger?*

But that dreamlike joy would very soon collide with reality.

What Chad didn't know, what no one knew, was that my depression was raging. Now, Chad knew about my past struggles with mental health, but he didn't know I was in full-blown active depression again. I didn't say anything to anybody because I didn't want people to be like, "Oh Lord! Here we go again." I definitely didn't want Chad to be questioning whether I was stable enough to be his wife. He'd never known me to be fully depressed, and I wanted to keep it that way. So, for about seven months, I faked it.

Have you ever left wet laundry in the washer too long? After some time it starts to stink, right? You can smell it down the hall, and you know what it is without even looking. And my dirty laundry was about to clear the room.

Between prepping for Coachella, trying to keep our engagement out of the media, and self-managing my dwindling mental health, my nerves were about shot. Then one day, Chad casually mentioned he wanted to get married in four months. *Four.* And I was like, *Four months? Like, one, two, three, four?*

Chad told me that yes, he wanted the wedding to take place in the amount of time it takes me to decide on which shoes I want to wear to an event. I remember one time he told me, "That ring on your hand is going to implode in four months unless we're married."

Obviously he was joking about the ring, but the man was serious about wanting to make me his wife reeeeal quick.

From Chad's perspective, he was just ready. He felt like *we* were just ready. At the time, he was working as a chaplain for the Steelers. He lived in Pittsburgh alone, and while we were dating, I went to visit him all the time. It was such a unique season for both of us, because we were really able to put in a lot of one-on-one time together. We were learning more and more about each other and growing. We got to play in a city that didn't really belong to either of us, so exploring Pittsburgh together brought us so much closer.

Chad was doing the math. *I want to get married; she wants to get married. I want a family; she wants a family. We've put in plenty of quality time together. We believe this is God's will. We ain't getting any younger. We're in love. We're engaged. Why wait?*

So I was like, *Okay, I guess Mindy Weiss can do anything.* Mindy is a world-renowned event planner, and I wanted her to do our wedding because she's like the fairy godmother of events and parties. She can plan a wedding in two weeks—that's how magical she is. So logistically, I knew it was possible. But in the back of my mind, I was thinking, *Four months?* I wanted us to get some more counseling. I wanted to enjoy being engaged. I wanted to move at a pace I was comfortable with. I didn't want more time to make sure he was the man I wanted to marry, because I knew that without a doubt. I just wanted more time to make sure we had the tools to make our marriage the best relationship it could be. I wanted to make sure we knew how to communicate, how to resolve conflict. Because I did not see healthy conflict resolution growing up and hadn't done a great job of it myself in past relationships.

I was stressed out. The man was excited to marry me, and somehow I ended up making that a negative in our relationship.

Chad's commitment to the Steelers ended, and I was still living in the cornfields of Illinois. I loved it there, and I thoroughly enjoyed my daily visits from the local deer, turkey, and other random wildlife. That's something people are always surprised to learn about me, that I love nature. I love living in the country with the trees and animals.

About that same time, we started to make a plan for where we'd live together once we were married. He was coming out of cold weather in Pittsburgh, and I was tired of the loooooong winters in Illinois, so we decided I'd get a place out in sunny LA since he was already out there doing spring training with the Dodgers. One thing he always told me, he always said, "I don't care if we live in the smallest, most run-down dump on earth, as long as I've got you and a little bit of sunshine."

But I had my concerns about listing my house. I had put the same property on the market before, and it never sold. So imagine my surprise (low-key panic) when I listed it on Friday and it sold the next Monday. I was like, *Wait! I wanted that to happen, but dang! That was fast.*

Everything seemed to be happening so fast. Way more quickly than I thought I'd have to, I packed up my home and moved to the West Coast.

Now, I had lived in LA before. Maybe for a year in the mid-2000s. And I hated it then. I would actually fly back home to Illinois for a week every month or so just to cleanse myself of the place. I had an apartment in a very trendy area during that time, and I honestly couldn't stand it or LA. But this time, I was moving to be with my fiancé. This time everything would be different, better. Right?!

Not if my depression had anything to do with it.

Once I got settled in LA, I could see the disease beginning to infect random places in my life. For example, I couldn't bring myself to buy furniture for my place. I just didn't have the desire to do it. Which is so unlike me—I love decorating and making places homey. But for some reason (ahem, depression), I didn't have the energy to do the things I used to love. I told myself I was just sad that I had to downsize so much. That it was normal to experience some feelings of grieving and sadness when you move. That I missed my family, the cornfields, and the small town I had left.

No one is a better liar than a depressed person in denial.

Later, Chad would tell me that this was the first sign that something deeper may have been going on with me. He'd say, "Babe, let's go shopping. Let's go get stuff for the new place." And I'd just shrug my shoulders at all his suggestions like I couldn't care less what kind of sofa we got or what color curtains hung in the bedroom. He was worried but afraid to ask me exactly what was going on.

Let me pause here and tell you a little more about Chad. Chad is the first to admit that he is a "fixer." He's a solutions guy. When Chad was fourteen, his parents divorced and he moved with his mom and sister. He became the man of the house before he had hair on his chest. Then, through a series of events that are personal to Chad's family,

No one is a better liar than a depressed person in denial.

Chad helped raise his two nephews, even moving them in for a time and being the father figure.

Chad is a human superhero. He'd never say that about himself, but he is. He swoops in. He saves the day. He figures out what needs to be done and he does it. Unfortunately, you can't "save" someone from depression. Especially when you don't even know that's what the person you love is suffering from. In the state I was in, I couldn't remove myself enough emotionally to see that Chad was trying to help me. Instead, it felt like he was patronizing me.

I would get so irritated when he offered support. He'd be like, "Let me make a call. Let me scramble some eggs. Let me handle this meeting." And I'd hear, "You can't get it together. See what I have to deal with? I have to do all this *for* you because you're incapable of doing it alone."

But that's not at all what Chad's intent was. He wasn't trying to be a parent to me; he was trying to be my partner.

Imagine that my mind is a big electric fan. On a good day, it whirls to life perfectly at the highest setting, humming right along as I go about life. On a hard day, it's like a fan on a lower setting. We're still getting the job done, but it takes a lot more time and effort. On my worst days, the fan has an electrical short. I keep plugging it in and unplugging it. Sometimes it'll huff and puff a few times, but others, no luck.

At this point in my life, the fan's blades had been bent all to heck. The cord was stripped. The plug was crooked from me trying to force it back into the outlet. And a small flame blew to life every time I tried to make it work. The best I could hope for was one of the bad days. I wasn't operating at maximum capacity, ever.

About a month after we got engaged, Chad and I had a disagreement. And it wasn't even over anything that important. Matter of fact, it was so very *not* important that I don't even remember what we were discussing.

For some reason, during the middle of the argument, I thought it'd be a good idea to take my ring off and slam it down. It was like I was saying, *See? I'm right and you're wrong. We ain't ready to get married yet. And you're rushing us into this before we are.*

I think that's the first time I took off my ring following a fight. And I am not proud to report that I ended up doing that multiple times over the next few months. I went from zero to a hundred if Chad sighed too loud. I was so on edge, looking for everything that was wrong or could go wrong. Being around me was like walking in a dark room full of bear traps. You never knew when one step was going to make me snap.

Looking back, I always regret that taking the ring off was my first move. I think about the sacrifice Chad made to get my ring, and how he saved up for ten years before he even met me, in faith that God was going to send him his wife. And then he proposes, and the woman he's engaged to takes it off every time they have an argument.

I can remember distinctly riding down the road and looking down at that ring. Why is the lighting in a car the best lighting to look at your ring? I don't know, but the sunlight was catching the diamond cuts *just* right. Chad was driving, and I was doubting my worth. I even took a picture—I was so unconvinced of my own worth that I had to document the moment to believe it was real. I was looking at it, counting my faults and imperfections, wondering how Chad could have chosen *me*. Believing lies that I wasn't good enough for that answered prayer.

What's so crazy is that Chad had no idea that the ring he'd given me had been the one I'd been wanting. Before we'd gotten engaged, I had taken a screenshot of a ring so I could drop a (not so subtle) hint to Chad about what I liked. Little did I know that Chad had already started designing the exact same ring. I should have looked at the ring as confirmation. Instead, I looked at it and thought, *Girl, bye! You don't deserve this!*

All I can tell you is that I was out of it. In my head, I viewed everything through the filter of, *This wedding isn't happening anyway because Chad is going to leave you or not fight for you. So you should end this thing before he does.*

I would tell him that, and he'd ask me why. What had he ever done to make me think for one second that he would leave me? I didn't have a good answer. I would say, "You deserve someone better. Go find her, but it isn't me."

I didn't have a good answer for my own questions, much less his.

"What do you have to be depressed about? You're about to perform at Coachella. You're about to reunite with your girls again. You're in rehearsals every day, and you're having a blast. You've moved to one of the most beautiful places in the world, Los Angeles. You've got your own place. You can't possibly be depressed again. You've overcome it. Right?"

It got to the point where every time Chad and I had an argument I felt like he didn't love me anymore. This started happening a lot. And I mean *a lot.* I felt unworthy of receiving what I'd prayed for. Because Chad was exactly what I had been praying for.

Like honestly, if I had to list the man's cons, they'd be that he farts too much and takes way too long to get to his point when explaining things. And . . . that's about it. So I was like, *Okay, God. We can work on those two things.*

But there were so many seeds of doubt planted in my mind. From my past, from the Enemy, from myself. And in my mind, I came into agreement with those doubts, repeating them to myself over and over again. Every time I told myself the relationship was doomed, I watered those seeds until I had this big ole lavish garden of doubt in full bloom.

By the time that following summer hit, I was completely bugging out. I was filming *Raven's Home* with Disney, and I just remember feeling like I was in complete darkness. I felt ashamed, lonely, and misunderstood. I was lost. I knew I needed a reset, but I didn't know how to do that. I knew my emotions were at a boiling point, but I didn't know how to turn down the heat.

I was sitting in hair and makeup on the set of the show, and the sweet little makeup artist could tell I was not okay. She was like, "Honey, what is going on?" And I just broke down. I was breaking down all the time, having crying fits for no reason. So I opened up to her and told her what I was going through. Sometimes it's easier to tell a stranger the truth than it is the people you love. I'll never forget how kind she was to me. She shared with me her own struggle with anxiety, and it really touched me that she was so vulnerable.

But listening to her also made me realize something very important. The current state of my anxiety and depression was far, far worse than the average person's.

Then, in July, I decided to get out of town. Chad was speaking at a camp, and I decided to drive up to surprise him there. He had no idea I was coming—I just showed up. And it was awesome. It was the same camp where he had prayed to receive salvation so many years ago. It just seemed like a place that would offer us respite—some refuge, some relief. And God used Chad in a huge way at the event. Hundreds of students gave their lives to the Lord there after he spoke that week.

After the camp Chad decided to bring his nephews to LA to visit my new place. The boys—who were really young men at the time, teenagers—are incredible. What happened on this visit had nothing to do with them. It had to do with me. I felt inadequate to host them. I know how loving, nurturing, and wonderful Chad's mom is, and I didn't feel like I was able to give them that. I didn't love my apartment. I don't cook. I was overly sensitive, and Chad and I ended up having a blowout argument. We did try to go to a counseling session during their visit. All I can say about its success is that we drove there together, but one of us left the appointment in an Uber.

Like a shaken-up bottle of champagne, your girl popped like a cork. I had said some pretty hurtful things to Chad along the way, but that visit, I got nasty. So Chad, completely sucker-punched by my reaction, had a friend come pick them up.

It was over. Chad and I were over. As soon as I realized what had happened, the bottom fell out for me. I spent the next couple of days on my sofa, vacillating between catatonic and hysterical.

In fact, it had gotten so bad that all I could think about was dying. If I ceased to exist, then I wouldn't have to feel the way I was feeling anymore. I wouldn't have to make everyone around me feel the way I felt I was making them feel. Everybody would be happier if I were just gone.

Have you ever exercised for a period of time, taken a break, then started back up again? It's almost like your body slides back into the routine. Your muscles redevelop, and you go through the motions like you've never stopped. That's called muscle memory. And the same concept applies to your mind. This is where those checking-in muscles I'd been slowly building started to come back to life.

Even if my mind wasn't functioning right, my spirit knew I wasn't being honest with myself about how sick my mind and heart had grown. I knew that the thoughts of suicide I was having were dangerous. Somehow, in the fog of despair and hopelessness, it was like my mind robotically went through the motions of checking in.

That was the night my pastor friend and his wife called me. See, I was supposed to be at an event with them, but I didn't show up. Didn't call or text. I was drowning, deep under water and incapable of swimming back to shore on my own.

"We know *you*," they told me. "This isn't *you*. You are a child of a King! You are dearly loved and cherished."

I honestly don't remember a lot from that night. I wasn't drinking or taking anything; I was just *that* disconnected from myself. I do know someone mentioned me checking myself in somewhere. And I knew that was probably the best idea because what I was doing wasn't working anymore. It had never really worked to begin with.

I decided to sleep on it. When I woke up the next morning, I was like, *Yup. Still feeling crazy.* That was when I knew it deep down in my bones. No matter how embarrassing, or inconvenient, or how dang expensive it was going to be, it was time to check myself in somewhere.

See, that's the thing about checking in. It's not always something you can do behind closed doors or in the privacy of a church or small group. Sometimes you have to check in publicly. You have to be willing to expose yourself a little to check in. You have to take a risk. Sometimes you'll have to disappoint people too. I was in the middle of filming a TV spot, and I think they had to reshoot the entire episode because I checked in. I think for me, disappointing people who were counting on me was the hardest part to accept.

But that check-in was one of the most important check-ins of my entire life.

Chapter Eight

I CALLED MY THERAPIST, AND WE BEGAN SEARCHING for treatment centers together. We found a place on the West Coast and made arrangements. Before I could talk myself out of it, I got in my car and drove myself to the facility. That drive was a blur. I just threw on a sweat suit and a hat and went. This is how out of it I was, y'all. I didn't pack a single thing. Not a pillow, toothbrush, or a pair of panties. I was in a bad way.

When I look back, I crack myself up. I didn't do the typical things I'd usually do before going out in public. I certainly didn't go to the spa and get my lip waxed or anything. I didn't get my eyebrows done. My hair was sticking up everywhere like a used Halloween wig. Alone, pretty ragged looking, but knowing it was the right thing, I checked myself in to a hospital.

One of the first things the staff did was take my phone so I couldn't contact anyone and they couldn't contact me—that would be too distracting for the healing that needed to be done. They did let me access my contacts list beforehand and write down a few emergency numbers. Of course, I had Chad's memorized. I wrote down Mom's, my manager's, my cousin's . . . the few people who would need to hear from me so they wouldn't think I'd been abducted or something.

Once inside the hospital, that frenzied, manic energy that had gotten me there evaporated. It was like I had been dog-paddling in the middle of the ocean for a week and I was finally on shore, able to catch my breath. I was given a room, and I immediately laid down. I just wanted to sleep. The staff came in every fifteen minutes to make sure I was still alive. I was just so tired. And I felt safe for the first time since I could remember.

One of the nicest people I met during my stay there was a nurse. When she found out I didn't bring any clothes with me, she ran to Target for me and loaded me up. So don't y'all worry, I had me some clean drawers!

There were so many brilliant people inside the facility. It wasn't like what you see in the movies: a bunch of drugged-up people wearing white, shuffling around like zombies. These people had stories and souls. These people mattered to God.

But there's always that one guy, right? One staff member was completely aloof with me. With other patients, he smiled and made small talk. But with me? Maybe he thought I was a spoiled, rich celebrity who wanted attention. Maybe he thought I was making up everything I said. But he made sure I knew he was *not* impressed with Michelle Williams. Honestly, it didn't hurt my feelings. It made me sad. Why not treat everybody the same? Maybe he was desensitized to certain types of people because he sees them so often. I don't know.

But his demeanor toward me definitely changed a few days later. Even *that* guy, in all his arrogant unaffectedness, showed me kindness after what happened next.

After being at the treatment center for a few days, I was contacted by my manager. There was an emergency. Somehow, TMZ had gotten word that I had checked myself into the hospital, and they were asking for a statement.

Now, TMZ asking for a statement was not a favor to me. They were going to run the story no matter what I said or didn't say. My giving them a statement was good for them because they had confirmation of my stay. But also, if I didn't give a statement, they would release whatever information they wanted without my input.

I spoke from the heart in my statement, even though I was broken by having to say it:

> For years I have dedicated myself to increasing awareness to mental health and empowering people to recognize when it's time to seek help, support, and guidance from those that love and care for your well-being.
>
> I recently listened to the same advice I have given to thousands around the world and sought help from a great team of healthcare professionals.
>
> Today I proudly, happily, and healthily stand here as someone who will continue to always lead by example as I tirelessly advocate for the betterment of those in need.
>
> If you change your mind, you can change your life.

Now that it was "out" where I was, I didn't know what to do. For years I had been championing mental health awareness, and then I end up in the hospital? I felt like a hypocrite. I felt like everyone I had tried to help over the years would be disheartened or disappointed in me.

The other unfortunate side effect of TMZ's actions was that I hadn't told my parents where I was yet. I had wanted to get a little steadier before I did that. So I was forced to call my mom and tell her what was going on long before I was ready. She was so concerned for me. She told me they would fast and pray for me, and I had no doubt she'd see to it. My mama—there is *no one* better in a crisis situation than she is.

The whole experience was turning out to be a disaster. I was so sad. So, so sad that I had reached out for help and couldn't even stay three days and focus on myself before a tabloid ran a Mack truck over my efforts. But more than that, I worried how it would affect other people who were afraid to ask for help. What message did it send to people that I had to make that statement and wasn't allowed to have privacy?

I really think that's what keeps many high-profile people from checking into a facility or seeking treatment from certain doctors— the threat of the media finding out and exposing them before they're ready to share that information with the world. Heck, I wasn't even ready to share it with my family yet!

To this day, I still don't know who leaked my check-in to the media. Maybe somebody told somebody they trusted, who told somebody they trusted, who told somebody they trusted. Only that last person wasn't trust*worthy*. It could have been another patient. It could have been the woman who served me those horrible powdered eggs at breakfast. I don't know. But the damage was done.

I sat in my room, not knowing if I should go or if I should stay. But when a nurse told me they had paparazzi hiding in the bushes with mega-zoom lenses so I needed to keep the blinds down and avoid the windows, I knew even if I stayed, I wouldn't be able to concentrate on the work that needed to be done. Not to mention the other patients' right to privacy.

So within eighteen hours of the news breaking, I checked out and went back to my place in LA.

But while I was still in the hospital, Chad got a call from our show's production company. That's how he found out where I was, through a business call. I was able to get in touch with him, and I asked him to come see me. God only knows why, but the man agreed. We sat together as I tried to explain and apologize for the last six or seven months of erratic behavior in the time frame of his two-hour visit. His poor nephews were still with him, and they had to sit in the parking lot of the hospital while we met.

When I got back to my place in LA, Chad didn't come right away. He was still with his family, and things were still extremely confusing for him. I really wasn't ready to face him again anyway. The first few days were a little bit of a blur. I was trying to get stabilized on my new medication and really not yet able to process all that had happened. But I am so blessed, because I came home to a community of people wanting to love on and check in with me.

The day I got home, Kelly made sure that her hair stylist was there waiting on me to do my hair. The girl who does my eyebrows was also there, ready to beat back the bushes cropping up on my face. Listen, I am a firm believer that doing things on the outside to make you feel better on the inside is a totally acceptable form of self-care. Because I for *sure* had a more positive outlook on life when those ladies left.

In the days following my public statement, I was blown away by the amount of love and encouragement I received. From my peers in the industry to a random mom in Idaho on Instagram, I read every message and felt the power of everyone's prayers. I mean, I got so many notes and emails from people that were absolutely supportive. To this day, people are very supportive. I'm very thankful for that.

When Chad did come, he was wonderful. He offered to cook for me, clean for me, and sit with me watching stupid shows. But later he would tell me he felt helpless. Which for him is the highest form of failure. He had given up everything for me. He had sold all his stuff and signed on to do the show full-time, so he didn't have a job to go back to. He didn't have a home to go back to. All he had now was a fiancée he didn't recognize and a phone ringing off the hook with people asking questions he didn't have answers for.

During that first visit, I spent a lot of time asking for forgiveness. Even though at the time I didn't fully grasp all that I'd put him through, I knew I loved him deeply and didn't want to lose him. Chad was confused; I think he even used the word *startled*. I had hurled some pretty vicious insults at him in our last argument, but I loved him and wanted to marry him?

I could tell he was reluctant, but Chad agreed to give me another chance.

That man sure knows how to take care of a woman. He was making sure I was eating every meal—breakfast, lunch, and dinner. He was just a champion. When a man sees you like that, that vulnerable, that broken, and he still wants to marry you, you'd think that would be enough to unearth the roots in that garden of doubt my mind had grown about us. But it wasn't.

It was probably three or four days after Chad arrived that we had to start back filming *Chad Loves Michelle*. After the news broke that I was in the hospital, Chad said his phone rang at least a hundred times a day. People from his world checking in. People from my world checking in. People from *our* world checking in. And the production company chiefly among them. Once I was out, the questions began to be directed at me too.

Honestly, I didn't want to resume filming, and Chad didn't want to either. I was fresh out of the hospital, and I had just broken up with the guy. We didn't see how it was possible. Legally speaking, however, we were informed that not only was it possible, it was mandatory.

So now I had a new dilemma. Do we pick up taping like those few days didn't happen? Or do we allow my stay in the hospital to become part of the story line? And I had people in my ear again, people telling me I *should* share. People telling me to use my hospitalization as a tool, use it to minister to people, use it to help people. Now, these weren't the same people I would be checking in with— these were other people. And had I been in a healthier position, I would have asked myself, *Now, are these folks who are bending your ear folks who know you, love you, and want the best for you?* The answer would have informed how much influence I allowed these "other" voices to have. But I never gauged the motives of those around me. I wasn't checking in with who I was checking in with, get me?

All I knew was, if I had to do the show, I sure wasn't going to hide what had happened. So when the cameras started rolling again, they caught me at my very lowest. They caught Chad and me at what was then our very lowest.

Sounds like fun, right?

Sounds like a recipe for a healthy relationship, right?

I hope my sarcasm is seeping through these pages, because it is glaringly obvious how bad an idea continuing the show was.

Needless to say, the relationship between Chad and me was stressed. Stressed isn't even a good word, actually. We were crumbling, splintering at the breaking point. The schedule for filming a reality TV show is enough to grind down anyone's mental health. Sometimes we'd get a call the night before or sometimes the day of to tell us to get ready. We'd go to our separate bathrooms, get washed up and dressed, and look at each other like, *What the hell are we doing?* Then we'd have a fourteen-hour day of filming just to go to bed and get another call the next morning.

Filming became a chore. And not a chore we enjoyed. It was like scrubbing nasty toilets. All I could think about the entire time was that Chad and I needed a break. We needed a break from everything just to be with each other. I remember so often Chad would say, "Michelle, I just need a date. Just one night to you and me." We'd get dressed up and drive somewhere together just to sit in the car in the parking lot. We were so exhausted. We barely had energy to lift a fork to our faces, much less to heal our relationship.

I needed to personally heal too. I wasn't going to be good for anybody—him, the show, me—until I addressed my mental health directly.

So you're thinking, *Michelle. Pull the plug on this thing!* And I'm with you. I hear you. But at the time it wasn't so crystal clear. There were some very real, very logical fears roaring between my ears. I was also worried about my life. I was worried about my career. I had already dipped out to go to the hospital; if I did go through the legal process required to quit the show, would I ever be seen as trustworthy in the industry again?

Then I'd look at Chad. And I'd tell myself I needed to get right for him. Was he wondering, *Who the hell did I propose to?* Probably! Then I'd go back down the rabbit trail of self-deprecation.

Why can't I just be happy?
Why can't I just be normal?
Why can't I get over this?

See, when you check in with others, you can't just listen to what's being said to you and take it as the right thing to do. You've got to ask yourself, *Is this wise?* You've got to ask God, *What does your Word say? What does the Holy Spirit tell me about this?* Running it through all three filters of checking in will give you the clearest, most rounded, and fullest view of which choices to make and which to avoid.

But because I wasn't there yet, to that level of checking in, I just jumped back into filming.

But here's the truth: I probably prayed more during that time than I ever have in my entire life. I would pray, *God show me what to do. Help me get better. Why can't I find joy in all you've given me? If you tell me what to do, I'll do it.* But I wasn't getting better, and I didn't feel like I knew what to do next.

Discerning God's will isn't always easy. It's really not, at least for me. There have been times when he has spoken to me so clearly that I'd bet my life on it. Then there are times it feels like I'm begging him for just a gentle nudge in one direction, and all I get is silence.

If you read in the Old Testament at all, you'll see some of the great prophets having these same struggles. Even David, the man after God's own heart, got frustrated by God's perceived silence. In the opening to Psalm 13, David's like, "Hey God! Remember me? How long do you plan on ignoring me? Are you thinking forever? Because I'm straight-up wrestling with my own thoughts over here, and I could really use your help!" (My paraphrase.)

But that's where faith comes in. That's where relying on intuition, that knowledge that feels like it's always been there because it's the Holy Spirit, comes in. And to be honest, I think God is okay with us wrestling with our own thoughts every once in a while. That's what makes us grow. That's what teaches us. That's where we find out what we're made of and where we need to improve.

And even though it frustrates us, hurts us, and sometimes scares us, God is comfortable with our discomfort. Because like any loving parent, God wants us to be the best version of ourselves. He wants more for us than what we'd choose for ourselves. And part of receiving that *more* means we have to experience the *less*. The silence. The suffering.

But we don't have to experience it alone.

Looking back, one of the biggest mistakes I made—and Chad would agree with this too—was the circle of people we had surrounded ourselves with. The truth is, we didn't have the right kind of people in our corner. And I'm not talking about everybody. I'm just talking about the people we were turning to and asking for advice.

Now, I want to stop here and take a minute to unpack this idea of checking in with others. Because it's important—critical, even. In fact, think of the approach of checking in with God, yourself, and others as a three-legged stool. There will be times when you lean more on one during different seasons of life, sure. But each leg is required to keep your butt off the ground.

So we have to get this right and find the correct people to be in our inner circle. During this time in my life, I had good people around me. People who loved God, sure. But I didn't have *the correct* people. Let me tell you what I look for now when I am choosing people to share my heart with and when I'm getting ready to listen to advice from someone.

1. **They love God.** Their faith is real. I see them privately and publicly walking out a faith that bears fruit. Are they perfect? Come on, nobody is. But these people are in the trenches of prayer, reading the Word, and pursuing God in a tangible way.

2. **They want what's best for me.** This is probably the most difficult quality to find in someone you can check in with. Someone who genuinely wants you to win, all the time, regardless of what it may cost them personally.

3. **They love me enough to tell me the truth.** If you're surrounded by people who are constantly nodding, you aren't maximizing the potential of your inner circle. You gotta have a few ladies in your corner saying, "Nah, sis. That ain't for you." You may have to give them permission to disagree with you (for example, not ripping off their heads when they offer a different perspective). But you have to be challenged in your friendships. If not, you're doing yourself a disservice.

When Chad and I disintegrated, we needed these types of people in our lives—people of depth to pick us up. We needed pillars. People to tell us we were doing too much of the wrong things and too little of the things that mattered.

If you're going to be checking in with others, you have to know who those others are and what they stand for. You need *safe* people. You need people who want you to win. Not just win in the way that benefits them, but win in a way that brings you closer to God.

If you're going
to be checking
in with others,
you have to
know who those
others are
and what they
stand for.

Chad and I didn't have those kinds of people in our circle. We had a lot of people who wanted to be around us, seen with us, and connected with us, especially when we were doing well. But when things got hard, when the cameras stopped rolling, when it stopped being convenient, they were nowhere to be found. They got very busy all of a sudden. Their texts stopped coming through. They stopped being available for dinners and coffees.

Here's one sign that you don't have the best people to check in with in your life. If your friends never ask you tough questions, they're not the right people. If your friends don't push you, sharpen you, or make you want to be better at least some of the time, they're not the right people.

But at the same time, you have to be the kind of person who can receive correction. You have to let your friends know that you welcome and invite their constructive criticism. Even if you have to send them a text once a month that says, "Hey, what's something I can get better at?" or, "What's it like to be my friend lately?"

Chad and I both had several people come up to us after our final breakup and say, "I wanted to say something. I wanted to speak up. I wanted to warn you." But they didn't. Maybe they felt like they couldn't. So we have to be clear. When it comes to people we want to check in with, we have to give them permission to tell us hard things.

One thing I will say is that since 2018, I have been way more intentional about my circle. I have had to get out and actually *look* for awesome friends instead of relying on life to provide friends for me. That means I've had to get uncomfortable at times. I've had to go to events and talk to people I didn't know. I've had to reach out over social media to people. Like, sliding into other women's DMs to try and be their friend. I've had to make myself a little vulnerable and say, "Hey. You seem like someone who knows a lot about God. You seem like you are really comfortable in your own skin. Do you wanna be my friend?"

It sounds almost silly, but some of my deepest friendships have been ones that I've sought out. I've hunted them down and looked for them. I've looked for people in the next season of life from me. I've looked for people who are something I aspire to be. I've looked for people who have things that I want. Not necessarily material things, but spiritual things. Character traits I want to possess. Emotional stability. Honesty.

I guarantee if I had the same circle around me back in 2018 that I have now, it would have been a completely different year.

It matters who you are checking in with. It could be the determining factor in whether you reach your full potential.

Chapter Nine

HAVE YOU EVER PLAYED THE WHAT-IF GAME?

What if . . .

- I had gone to college instead?
- I had ended that relationship sooner?
- I had listened?
- I hadn't listened?
- I had said yes?
- I had said no?

Here's the thing about the what-if game: we're all losing. Okay? Nobody wins when you try to live in a moment that never was and never could be. But we're human, right? And it's human nature to think back on big decisions and wonder a little bit. Like, how would my life be different? How would *I* be different?

One of the biggest what-ifs I've had to stop tormenting myself over is when I felt like God told me to take a year to myself, but I didn't.

I was at a women's retreat learning about Esther. If you've read the Bible, you know who Esther is. Even if you haven't read the Bible, you may have heard her story. Because she was bad. Like, the good kind of bad.

Basically, Esther was this beautiful Jewish woman who ended up marrying a Persian king named Xerxes in a process that was very similar to the show *The Bachelor*. (Sidenote: You should read the Bible, y'all.

There's some entertaining stuff in there!) But Esther had more than just her looks. She was fiercely loyal, brave as hell, and had a fiery faith. After marrying Xerxes, she actually ended up exposing and putting an end to a plot to massacre the Jewish people (her people) in her nation. Yeah, so Esther was one of those OG Independent Women.

But before Esther married her king, she spent twelve months preparing to meet him. I won't get into my personal opinion on Old Testament traditions, culture, or the attitude toward women at this point in history, but it was customary for them to spend a year "beautifying" themselves before they were introduced to the king, who was in the market for a new queen.

I was sitting at this retreat, and I was really intrigued by this idea of preparation. A full year to do nothing but get your outside soft, glowing, and gorgeous. And I was struck by this idea of *What if I took a year to get my inside right? To get my heart soft, glowing, and gorgeous?*

It was like God whispered, "If you will give me one year of your life, just *wait* and see what I'll do with it."

I was like, *Yes Lord! Let's do this. No dating for a year. No boyfriends. Take some time off working so much. Just you and me, God. You and me! A year of internal beautification!*

Well, four months into the twelve, I met Chad. And you know what happened next.

What if I had told Chad to wait? To just hit me back at the end of that year? To maybe stay my friend, but nothing more for the next eight months? If he couldn't wait, fine. If he found someone else in the meantime, he wasn't meant for me anyway. If I had given God the year he asked for, how would our story have been different? How would *I* have been different? What if?

But like I said, ain't no sense in trying to live in a moment that never was.

I also wonder "what if" about our choice to return to filming. What if I had just put my foot down and said, "No. I don't care who gets mad or inconvenienced, I have to put my mental health first"?

※

I got out of the hospital, we went back to filming, and I tried to pick up the broken pieces of my life and sort of tape them back together for the time being.

In the middle of that mess, I got the opportunity to get back on the Broadway stage in a Tony Award–winning revival of *Once on This Island*. I was offered the role of Erzulie, the goddess of love. And despite my own current handicap in that department, I jumped at the chance to be distracted by my passion for theatre.

The new plan was: ignore my breakdown, make everyone happy, throw myself into a very work-heavy role, and hope for the best. Sounds solid, right? (It's okay. I'm rolling my eyes at myself too.)

So instead of checking in and asking myself tough questions, checking in with God and lining up my thoughts with his Word, checking in with my trusted friends, I shushed my common sense into silence by repeating a lot of positive statements.

Yo, Michelle. You have a lot to be thankful for. You have an engagement. You're going to get married! You're filming a show for the Oprah Winfrey Network, which is one of the best networks to work with. You also have a Broadway show that's going to be amazing. After you and Chad get married, you get to live for six months together in New York. How fun is that going to be? Y'all don't have kids yet, but you're going to have a blast trying to create some kids in New York City on Broadway.

Get. Over. Your. Depression.

All my blind optimism was like putting a couple of Band-Aids over a heart that needed triple bypass surgery.

I should have been resting. I should have been healing. Chad and I should have been lying prostrate before Jesus. We should have been in prayer, not in hair and makeup. We should have been making sure our relationship was strong, not making sure our relationship was a ministry. Yes, taking care of ourselves should have come before trying to take care of anyone else.

And if the reality show was meant for us, then it would have been there for us when we got through doing what we needed to do to make sure our relationship was healthy. I'm not blaming the show. But it cranked up the heat on a relationship that was already in a broiler situation.

Meanwhile, back on planet Real Life, I had lines to learn for *Once on This Island.* Usually I get about six weeks to spend with a Broadway script before I perform, but for this show, I got two. Two weeks. So at that point I was like, *What else y'all need? World peace? A clean energy solution? Because apparently life thinks I'm capable of miracles.*

One of the most stressful parts about being in a Broadway show are the critics. Let me tell you now. There ain't a profession on the planet reviewed more harshly than being an actor on Broadway. And I've got some pride. I didn't want to suck. I take my craft very seriously, especially theatre. It was just so hard trying to do both shows at the same time. I never paused, never asked myself, God, or anyone else if what I was doing made sense. Probably because subconsciously I already knew the answer. I just kept on plowing through, trying to be Superwoman and failing.

December, the month of the show, came, and with it a snap in all the back-breaking bending.

I was in the middle of a phone conversation with Chad, and I don't even remember what we were arguing about. He made a comment that landed on me like a vat of hot lava. He said, "I can't do this emotional roller coaster anymore."

I heard, "I can't do *you* anymore. I can't do this relationship anymore. I don't want you anymore."

To say I lost it is a grave understatement. Later I would learn that what I experienced next was a true psychotic break—worse in some ways than the episode in July that sent me to the hospital. All I know is, I blacked out and responded manically. I got on Instagram and posted this big breakup message, saying my engagement was over and wishing Chad the best in his future without me. It took me about a month to be able to go back and read the post. I was with one of my friends, and I was like, "Um, I did that? I said that? I wrote that?!"

They were like, "Yeah, sis. You were out of control."

Again, to be in Chad's position and to read of the breakup on my Instagram story, I can't imagine how humiliating it was for him, for his family.

The emotional tornado spinning around in my head leveled me for the next couple of days. I don't really know how to describe it other than to say I felt either drunk or hungover, but I wasn't drinking. I was so tired, so sluggish, but all I could do was sleep. I wasn't making sense when I tried to communicate. And if I did communicate, I wasn't myself. I was acting as if I'd been possessed by either a zombie or an ax murderer, depending on the hour.

It wasn't long before people started coming into town to put eyes on me. One of my sisters flew in. A couple of friends. And my cousin Brittany. It's still a blur, but I knew everyone was worried. I wanted to tell them I was going to be okay, but I honestly didn't know. I was sinking in the quicksand of my hysteria, and I wasn't even fighting against it. I couldn't.

A few people have told me about conversations I don't even remember having.

My manager came to see me. Her goal was to try and remove me from the situation physically. Kind of like, *Let's get Michelle away from the scene of the crime.* Because I was acting very much like I was in a state of shock. She suggested I get out of New York, go somewhere warm, maybe. But I refused to leave. She told me later that I said, "I can't leave because Chad is coming. Chad is coming back." She said she broke down crying because she had to be the one to tell me. She was like, "No, Chad is not coming back."

Later on, Kelly would tell me something similar. She said she called me and that she prayed for me. But get this: she said I was so mean to her. I was like, "Kelly, I was mean to *you*?" She told me that I was plain awful to her, even when she was praying for me.

It's not funny at all, but I kind of have to laugh. Because I genuinely don't have any memory of this. Have you ever talked in your sleep or sleepwalked and then woke up to hear stories of all the crazy things you did and said? That's how it was, except your girl was awake. And this all happened over a few days, not one night. *That's* how out of it I was.

Like I said, my cousin Brittany had come to check on me, and she just took over. Thank God for that. Because the only thing I could have taken in that moment would have been a tranquilizer. She packed up my apartment in New York and brought me back home with her to Atlanta. I don't even know how I got the strength to put clothes on, go to the airport, check in, and get on a plane. But I came to Atlanta, and I've been here ever since.

Looking back, do I blame depression for ending my engagement? Do I blame the imbalance of chemicals in my brain? Do I blame the Enemy? Do I blame myself?

The short answer is yes. All those things played a role in the loss of my engagement.

However.

We all have a personal responsibility to make choices that protect what we value. And regardless of where the most blame lies, if I ever have the chance again to be engaged, I will guard my relationship at all costs by guarding my mental health at all costs.

The months that followed that December 2018 breakup (and breakdown) were bleak. The word I really want to use is *hell*, because that's how it felt. Like my insides were just on fire. From pain, regret, shame, humiliation, fear. January, February, March: all hell. Have you ever broken a dish or poured out a bag of sugar on the floor by accident? Just really made a mess and wondered how you'd ever clean it all up or make it right? That's where I was. I was just like, *What have I done. What in this world have I done?*

For a while I was still very much underwater. I slept a lot. More than I thought was humanly possible, actually. I couldn't eat much. I was staying with my cousin and her husband in their home, and I would just stay locked in my room a lot. I worried. I worried what people thought about me. What Chad's family thought about me. What Chad thought about me. There wasn't much contact between us at all during those days, though we exchanged a few messages. He was very cold, and he had every right to ice me out. He was scared too. And just as hurt as I was.

Slowly, with time and prayer, the searing pain faded to a dull ache. I remember one day I got up and was sick of myself. Sick of being pitiful and sick of being sick. I looked in the mirror and said out loud, "It's time to get tough. You can and will do this."

I'd been through bad breakups before. I knew the pain, like most emotional pain, was temporary. I reminded myself daily that my recovery was on me. Slowly, jagged piece by jagged piece, I walked around the wreckage of my life and started picking up the shards to see what could be salvaged. *Can this be saved? How should I dispose of this part over here? Does this need a repair, or should I just let this one go?* Searching for a way to rebuild something that resembled a future.

Honestly, one of the best things I did during that time was to start working out again. I'd get out of my cousin's house for an hour or two, get a sweat going, then come back. I started small like that. Real small. Like, walking-on-the-treadmill small. But that's okay. Humility is an incredibly strong teacher as much as it is anything else.

Early in the year, I was invited to go to a conference called Healing the Heart in Hiddenite, North Carolina. It was there that I took a big step toward healing. I confirmed that I had experienced some critical unmet needs as a child, and those unmet needs were *still* wreaking havoc in my adult life.

I also stayed away from men. Not just for a few weeks. For an entire year. The year 2019 was the first time in my adult life that I wasn't attached to a relationship. Listen, I know that leaning into a male relationship—even one labeled a friendship—is so tempting when you're feeling sad, rejected, or embarrassed. But for me, I felt like I'd be robbing myself of precious emotional margin—margin I needed to fully heal and recover.

On their own, these little steps led me down a path of healing. They felt small. But they were big. But it wasn't just simple like that. I had setbacks. I had bad days and bad weeks, even. But I knew the battle I needed to win wasn't with Chad, the media, a production company, or some grumpy old theatre critic. The battle I was facing was raging inside of me, inside my own mind. I knew I had to live, to think, to check in in a radically different way.

I've taken breaks from work from time to time, but never this intentionally. I took time for *me*. Time to press pause on outward progress in order to press play on inward progress. For the first time in twenty years, I wasn't concentrating on my music or my career.

Of course, I had heard the whisper of fear asking what pressing pause would cost me. *Will I fade into irrelevance? Will I miss out on that comeback opportunity? Will I ever pick up the microphone again?*

But regardless of what it cost me to check in, I had come to realize it was a bargain compared to checking *out*, to being swallowed up by the depression that constantly lurked in the backdrop of my life.

Later in 2019, I was on a reality television series on Fox called *The Masked Singer*. Hosted by Nick Cannon, with panelists Jenny McCarthy, Ken Jeong, Robin Thicke, and Nicole Scherzinger, the premise of the show is that a bunch of celebrities (singers and non-singers) put on full-body costumes and face masks that completely disguise any distinguishing characteristics of the contestants'

Regardless of what it cost me to check in, I had come to realize it was a bargain compared to checking out.

identities. Then, competitors face off by performing popular songs all while trying to remain anonymous.

First, let's talk about what you really want to know: Was it truly a secret that I was on the show? Yes! Honey, I was lying to everybody, even my mama. I got the call in July and didn't get "unmasked" until December. I lied for months and months. But this is part of what I do; I keep performances under wraps. Sometimes I wonder why anybody believes a single word that comes out of my mouth when it comes to work!

I remember in 2013 when Destiny's Child made a surprise appearance at Beyoncé's halftime show for Super Bowl XLVII. My phone was ringing off the hook with folks asking, "'Hey, are y'all doing the halftime show?"

"Nope, I don't know what you're talking about." But I'd be on a plane headed to rehearsals.

And can we talk about those rehearsals for just a minute? It had been a *while* since your girl had done choreography on that level. I'd been doing Broadway and, of course, performing my own stuff, but preparing for a halftime show requires *months* of intense rehearsals. I think B had a good six months in ahead of that performance.

So here I am, all sore and icing myself, and people are like, "Michelle, what have you been doing? You doing CrossFit now? You doing a new workout regimen? Why are you limping? Why are you icing your rear end?"

Couldn't say a word.

So, heading into *Masked*, I knew how to keep that kind of a secret. In fact, while the show was airing live, I was in a Christmas musical called *A Snow White Christmas*. All the kids from that show were constantly running up and asking me, "Michelle, are you on *The Masked Singer*?" And I was like, "Nope, I'm here in North Carolina with you guys!" Then they'd beg me to come into their room and watch *The Masked Singer* with them just so they could see my reaction to the performances.

Either kids are smarter than adults or I'm not as good at lying to them, because they definitely knew it was me despite my constant denials.

All that to say, my experience on *The Masked Singer* was nothing short of incredible. That time I had taken for myself, it had actually made a difference.

So when I got the call to take the stage again, not as Michelle Williams, but as a beautiful, ethereal, iridescent butterfly, you'd better believe I was all about it. I get to do what I love again, and I don't have to do it as myself? I can be whoever (or what-animal-ever) I want to be on that stage? I'm in. So about halfway through 2019, I agreed to do the show.

Speaking of butterfly, let me take a quick second to talk about the second thing y'all want to know: What was it like performing in that costume?

I've worn all manner of costumes, boots, heels, and props, but never have I had to sing and dance in a full-on headdress that covered my entire face and neck. I could barely see a thing! I would have to lift my head at a certain angle to move the eye slits so I could peer over the edges of them. *No pressure nailing the choreography, Michelle. You'll probably only break a couple of bones if you trip in these boots. Maybe just a toe, if you're lucky.*

But that costume was so fierce. There were a few other options I could have chosen, like a giraffe or something. But that butterfly spoke to me the moment I saw it.

After the airing of me being unmasked, three people who don't even know each other hit me up to say, "Hey, that butterfly costume was such a right choice. You really are a new person, a new creation. It's been amazing watching you change into who you are today."

And they weren't saying anything bad about who I had been in the past, but they'd seen me walk the road of healing and growing over the last couple of years, and they were excited to see how far I'd come.

I've got to be honest with y'all, though. During those calls, I was sitting on the other end of the phone shrugging, like, *I just thought the butterfly was cute.*

It's true! I hadn't envisioned this grand entrance onto the stage as an unveiling-type moment—a new Michelle emerging like a golden butterfly forged from a cocoon of fiery trials and tribulations.

Nope, I just wanted to look awesome. Wish I had some nice little bow to tie on the costume situation, but that's it. It was vanity.

Moving right along.

The outfit was glorious, but listen, I almost passed out from the heat one time. I thought to myself, *But you know what, Michelle? You may be laid out on the floor in front of a live and national TV audience, but you'll still be looking fire when TMZ runs that article with a photo of you mid-faint.*

Alas, I didn't win any awards. Heck, I didn't even win the show, but I can honestly say that *The Masked Singer* was one of the best things I've ever done in entertainment.

Why is that?

Sure, it felt nice to be affirmed by people's feedback, especially after taking a break from performing for most of the year. And after being unmasked, it was like waking up to an entirely different social media audience. People were being so *nice*.

I didn't know Michelle had chops like that.

Somebody bring that girl some flowers!

Michelle, we need a jazz/soul album from you!

So, yeah. It felt good. You've got to be bionic to not enjoy affirmation like that. But there was more to it.

Usually before a performance, I'm a little stressed. Even though I go into makeup and wardrobe immediately once I arrive on set, I try not to go into any studio looking like a wet cat that needs a nap. But for *Masked*, I rolled up looking whatever type of way I looked when I woke up.

And when I stepped on that stage in full costume . . . baaaby, let me tell you. I felt good. I felt better than good, actually. I wasn't worried about what people would expect when I sang, because they wouldn't know it was me. I wasn't concerned with trying to replicate or even top my Destiny's Child performances, nor did I dread hitting a sharp note just to wake up to read, "See, that's why she's not a lead vocal," all over the internet.

The result of this level of confidence? Your girl straight killed it on *Masked*! While it does feel low-key boastful to say that to you, would it be better if I lied? Nope. And after all I've failed at in the pages of this book, it sure feels good to hold my head up and tell you that I hit every note, step, and finger flick all while dressed like a huge butterfly who *couldn't even see.*

One detail from *The Masked Singer* that I didn't tell you about is the moment I got unmasked. You can watch it online if you google it, but when host Nick Cannon removed my headdress, tears sprang into my eyes. I cried. Personally, I'm not much of a crier. Especially on national television, but I couldn't help it. Truth be told, I was brought to tears after every one of my performances on that show.

I had convinced myself the world no longer wanted or needed my voice. I had labeled myself as used, tired, and done. In my mind, *Michelle* was done, but I wasn't really sure how to just be *Tenitra*.

And in that moment, I was both. I had given a Michelle-worthy performance, but I had gotten to do it my way, as me: Tenitra.

I have had an incredibly blessed life, for sure. And I'm so thankful for all the Lord has done for me. But being a celebrity going through a public breakup and breakdown is just rotten. Your darkest, most private moments are broadcast for the entire world to feast on.

But when I was unmasked, I had a sudden realization: I had agreed to do the show because I didn't have to be *me* on stage. But also, I needed to be *me* again.

When I was performing with a mask on, I was wild and free. I didn't have a care in the world. It was just me, the microphone, and the people who were cheering for me. There were probably people there who didn't love what I was doing, but I didn't see them because they couldn't see me. They couldn't label me based on anything besides the sound of my voice.

It was awesome.

Honestly, earlier that year, I thought I'd put my microphone down for the last time. I thought, *I'll just take a step back from the spotlight. I'll share my story. I'll help others through their depression. Maybe I'll become a mentor or even a counselor of some sort.* I thought I'd never sing on stage again.

Remember those labels we talked about earlier in the book? Well, I went ahead and labeled myself as finished in the music industry. Not because I wanted to be finished, but because I labeled my gift as useless; my gift that God has uniquely given to me.

Maybe this has happened to you.

Maybe you used to volunteer at your church in a certain ministry that you loved and thrived in. Maybe you gave countless hours to this role, sacrificed, stayed up late at night, fought for, and gave so much of yourself for it. But then something happened and you stopped. Someone hurt your feelings, or church leadership changed, or maybe you were even asked to step down. If you were to check in with yourself, you'd see that you're still wearing a lot of false labels as a result.

Or maybe you used to be married, but now you're not. Being someone's wife gave your life a sense of stability. It gave you a certain assurance about the future that you no longer have. Now that you're separated or divorced, you aren't sure what your identity is. You've had to remove some labels you loved and replace them with ones that represent your worst fears. You aren't sure how to check in with yourself because you're not even sure who *yourself* is anymore.

Or maybe, like me, one of life's heartbreaking disappointments ripped every meaningful label off your body so quick and mean that now you just feel raw. Maybe some of those labels were picked off in stages.

Didn't get the promotion.

Another negative pregnancy test.

Parents sided with her again.

Uninvited to the party.

Rip. Rip. Rip. Rip.

Or maybe those meaningful labels were snatched away from you all at once. Mine was the loss of a relationship and decided future. Maybe you have become estranged from a parent or sibling after a falling out. Or someone you love passed away. Or maybe life just hasn't turned out like you thought it would, and with each letdown you've experienced, who you think you are has changed, lessened.

For whatever reason, you've labeled your gift as useless—you've labeled yourself as useless.

Not long ago, I was in talks to be a regular host on a nationally syndicated talk show. And I was excited. I thought, *This is the next natural step for my career. This is how I will continue to contribute to society and share my story.* I truly thought I would get the opportunity.

But I didn't.

Want to know why? Because I'm single. I'm unmarried.

After that letdown, I was devastated. Just because I don't have a husband doesn't make my experiences as a woman, an American, a believer, and an artist less relevant. It was like they took the *She Matters* label right off my heart and replaced it with a huge *Forever Single* stamp on my forehead.

Months later, I could take a step back from the situation and see that this particular show wanted a well-rounded cast. They wanted married and unmarried hosts, and I just happened to tilt the balance in the wrong direction. The person they chose instead of me is a great girl and she's absolutely killing it.

Let's go back to what-ifs.

There is one good thing what-ifs can do for us if we leverage them the right way. If we can allow our what-ifs to inform us and not torture us, we can actually gain wisdom from that nagging feeling that creeps into our minds every time the past comes up.

So, what *if* I had given God a year to prepare my insides—my heart, my spirit, my mind—before dating Chad?

What if I had taken a break after the hospital? What if I hadn't overcommitted my time with the reality show and the Broadway show . . . oh, and threw in planning a wedding Chad and I had both waited half our lives for?

You know, Chad and I were in survival mode after my hospitalization. What if we'd gone away? Just gotten out of town together? We still loved each other. He didn't want to leave me. I didn't want to leave him.

I don't know. But in the future, when I think I am hearing the voice of God, I will do everything I can to check in with that thought before dismissing it. I will do my due diligence and share that feeling and thought with someone else. I'll run it by them. By someone who loves God and has a life that reflects a life I would want in the future. I'll check in.

Instead of letting the what-ifs choke the life out of me, I'm learning to use them as a lesson. To prevent me from making similar choices that lead to similar regret.

See, there are people who say they have no regrets in life. They also say that regrets are what made them who they are. And I see so much truth in that. I feel that. But at the same time, I want to become a person who learns lessons *without* regret. I want to be the kind of person who uses the wisdom God offers us daily to prevent future regret. And yes, I know I can't live the rest of my life without any regret, but I can do a few things to minimize the potential for hurt and pain.

For one, I've learned to never let myself get so busy again.

What if I hadn't kept so busy that I traded in my mental health for a check in a box that only I cared about? But that's a habit I got into without even knowing it. My entire life, I've been busy. Just doing stuff, you know? Singing in the choir. Serving in the church. Reading the Bible. Practicing certain harmonies. Making that daily phone call to my parents. Going to the gym. Wiping down all the counters. Wiping them down again.

I think being busy is something we can all relate to. Everywhere I go, people look busy. I was in the drive-through at Hardee's getting a biscuit the other day, and there was a woman in the parking lot putting on mascara, eating, talking on the phone, and feeding her toddler. I wanted to step out of my car and salute this lady.

Life is stressful. Not just work, family, the future, and our relationships. It's *all* stressful.

Don't you feel this? You look on Instagram and see someone's story. They've done prayed, worked out, enjoyed a breathtaking sunrise, juiced, made a gorgeous poached egg, cleaned out their closet, donated to charity, checked off their to-do lists, contoured their face, and met girlfriends for brunch, and you ain't even got the sleep crust out from the corner of your eyes yet.

You see that and you're automatically stressed out. *I should be doing more. I should be accomplishing more. I should at least pretend I've got it together.*

Do you ever feel like your boss thinks she's the only person in your life who is allowed to need something from you? Or that your kids think you just sit around all day and watch television and eat bonbons? Do you ever get those passive-aggressive texts from family members?

Saw your sister yesterday. Can't remember the last time I saw you. What do you look like, again?

Or how about the questions. If there's a life milestone you've yet to complete, that's all anybody wants to know about. When you gonna bring a man home? When y'all going to get engaged? When's the wedding? Aren't y'all ready for a baby? Have you not bought a house yet? You're still working there? I thought for sure you'd be done with that place by now.

It's like, *Dang, Aunt Tanya. I just came over for some banana pudding, not an FBI-worthy interrogation.*

And you walk away just feeling so completely stressed out. *I'm not doing enough, so I must not be enough. I feel like I'm doing the best I can, but I'm obviously failing. I have to find a way to do more. To be more.*

So we're already busy just doing life. Just keeping all the plates spinning, right? Then we get on social media, go to work, or see our family, and we automatically feel like we're not doing enough. So we get even busier. After a while, that level of living is going to take its toll—just like it did on me. We can't run on constant mental and emotional overload and not expect it to affect our hearts in a real and lasting way.

The thing is, the impact of busyness and a high-demand life isn't always clear. We're probably too busy to notice. But if you were to check in with how you're doing balancing your current schedule, you might be like I was.

- You're constantly irritated or on edge.
- You can't stop feeling like something bad is about to happen.

- You have trouble sleeping or staying asleep. Or, you sleep way too much and never feel rested.
- You either can't eat at all or you can't stop eating.
- You feel like you can't enjoy anything because you're worried what's going to happen next.
- You feel panicked a lot and can't pinpoint why.
- You feel like a big disappointment because as much as you want to do it all and do it well, you aren't. You can't.

It's rough, right? These are all signs of real anxiety. Just one is difficult, but a combination of them all? It's a wonder we aren't all walking around in straitjackets. Instead, we tell ourselves, "That's just how it is." We tell ourselves that we're the only ones who are struggling, the only ones who can't get it together.

One of the reasons I love the Bible is because it's real stories about real people. One of Jesus' followers named Peter was giving advice to a church that was having some trouble. And I don't mean they didn't have time to get a fresh eyebrow wax. These people were enduring some really serious religious persecution. Talk about anxiety, talk about stress. Here's what Peter said to them: "Cast all your anxiety on him because he cares for you" (1 Peter 5:7 NIV).

Other translations of this verse say, "Cast all your cares" or, "Cast all your worries." We don't use the word *cast* this way a whole lot, but it just means to throw. To toss. Peter told them to cast their anxiety away. To throw it, to toss it.

Maybe little sayings like this make you want to roll your eyes. It's like when you're frustrated or worried and somebody says something like, "Let go and let God." Or, "Don't worry, be happy!" Or, "It'll be okay." "Toss your worry away"? Really? How's that going to help me sleep tonight? How's that going to get my boss off my back? How's that going to make my parents stop harassing me?

It feels like the verse is just telling us to magically not feel stressed, and we know that's not possible. We want to *do* something. So, we worry. We have the same conversation over and over in our minds. We check to-do lists, scroll through our phones, or text our friends to complain about how busy we are.

But that's not the point of the verse.

My uncle used to take us fishing all the time. I didn't like it much; it was always freezing. Plus, I was garbage at baiting the line. My uncle actually used little hot dogs as bait, and I just remember how bad it all smelled. But after putting your bait on the hook, you have to cast your fishing line into the water. Now, I've always been lanky, with long arms and long legs. And casting out a fishing line is not something a lanky preteen girl is going to nail the first time around. Or the second. Or the third. In other words, it took practice.

This is what Peter is telling us: it takes practice. It takes practice to release the hold we have on our stress and anxiety. But God wants us to. He wants us to because he loves us. Because he cares. What Peter said is a big deal. Because—ahead of his time—Peter knew that stress, anxiety, and fear are a big deal.

So, back to me. And all my *not* casting of my cares.

My whole life, I had my little list of what I thought a good daughter was, a good employee was, even of what a good Christian was. Those lists ruled my life. If I crossed everything off, then I was okay. I was a good, acceptable person. If I didn't check all those boxes, then I was not a good person. I was actually a *bad* person. Instead of casting my cares on God, I held on to my cares. I embraced my cares. My cares were my security. One of the many problems with this way of thinking is that it gives my lists power that only God should have. I'm serving these lists, not God.

Because when Jesus died on the cross for me, he checked the only boxes that mattered:

- Redeemed
- Forgiven
- Whole
- Pure
- Blameless
- Good
- *His*

Instead of checking in with my own lists, I've learned to first check in with God's. Instead of saying, *How am I doing today in life? Who is happy with me? Who is mad at me? What have I done career-wise? What's my relationship status?* It's, *Okay, let's start with the baseline of what God has already accomplished on my behalf.* I'll even write it down, what God's list is for me. Even if it's hard. Even if it's annoying to me. Like, *Yeah, I'm redeemed. But I still ain't got a husband.* I'll still say it; I'll remind myself of his list. Because it's done, it's all checked off.

I'm learning to be honest.

Because, sure, maybe I couldn't have predicted the way the chemicals in my brain were going to interact or how the reality show was going to play out. Maybe I couldn't have anticipated certain insecurities rearing their ugly heads time and again, but I could have opened my mouth and talked about it. I could have said something like, "Chad, I don't feel like myself." Or, "Something isn't right." Or even called my therapist and said, "This is more than the normal anxiety and depression I'm used to feeling." I could have sent a text, a DM, an email, something.

We have no reason to allow ourselves to suffer in silence. And look, I understand the hesitation. I understand not wanting friends to roll their eyes and say, *Here we go again*. Because if that's what's holding us back, that's pride. How prideful are you gonna feel rolling up to the psychiatric ward because you were "too healed" to have a relapse? Because let me tell you, honey, I redefined the words *walk of shame* heading into that hospital. I didn't even care that I looked like I just walked in fresh off a plane crash. Because I had let it get to a true life-or-death situation.

I will say that I never set out to be *dis*honest. I never came up with a master plan to hide my depression. In fact, I thought I was very openly a mess. If you spent any time around me and saw my level-ten reactions to level-one problems, I was of the mind-set that everybody pretty much knew. I thought it was obvious. But it wasn't, not the complexity of it or the severity of it during 2018.

That's because there's a difference between being transparent and being vulnerable. It's a very important difference that cost me plenty of relationships, even friendships, along the way. See, I have no issues being transparent. Because with transparency, there's still a little bit of control. You can say, "Michelle, you seem a little off. Is everything okay?" I'll be transparent even to say, "Yeah, I'm going through some stuff right now. You know, it's hard, but God is good! I'll be okay!" I don't risk anything when I respond that way.

But when you're vulnerable, you don't have that kind of control. It's not pretty, and sometimes it doesn't feel like God is good. You know what I mean? When you're vulnerable, you don't care if your partner knows that you're frustrated they forgot to ask how that meeting went. Or that you're excited they called. You don't care if they know you're full of fear and doubt and worry. Or full of love, anticipation, and awe.

I'd say the biggest difference in being transparent and being vulnerable is that when you're vulnerable, no one has to ask you the tough questions because you are offering the truth freely. Transparency is simply offering information; vulnerability is revealing the thoughts behind your words and actions.

And y'all, I know it's tough. I know checking in with anyone in a vulnerable way is hard. Like, I'm never going to be with a man and say, "I just feel really insecure right now because you haven't said anything about this new way I'm doing my makeup," and that just be a breeze. Vulnerability is going to cost you a little something every time because it's human nature to hide our weaknesses. It just becomes our habit.

Guarding the truth was my crutch for so long. I don't want to talk about how hard my childhood was, because I don't want to hurt my parents and I don't want people to feel sorry for me. I don't want to talk about how let down I felt after Destiny's Child's disbanded, because I don't want to sound petty or like I'm not over it. I don't want to admit that I've been so frantic to be loved that I've chosen the wrong men, because I don't want to look stupid or desperate.

Being transparent was my crutch.

We do this in lots of areas—not just when it comes to being vulnerable. We get in a habit of doing things that feel good but aren't good. These are our coping mechanisms, the crutches we use instead of taking risks and checking in.

These things become second nature to us. Something we do without even thinking about it. For me, figuring out my "crutches" was a critical part of learning to check in. Because you can't check in until you're honest with yourself about the way you're living.

Have you ever noticed that? How you can get stuck in a pattern of doing something so much that you don't even realize you're doing it? We can do it in small ways. For example, you find yourself saying the same things over and over in conversations. Stuff like, "I mean," or, "You know," or you say "Umm" sixty times every time you're trying to tell someone a story. We do this to help us out when we aren't exactly sure what we're saying or to fill in pauses.

The problem is, very rarely do we feel like we have habits or behaviors we're stuck in. Not many of us would be bold enough to admit, "You know what? I feel like I'm trapped in these behavior patterns, and I can't get out of them." We just think it's how we're wired. Or we'll justify them.

We make excuses. Instead, we notice the circumstances that pushed us toward the behavior.

Well, I had to have that extra glass of wine tonight because work was insane. Instead of saying, *I didn't come prepared for that meeting, and that's why I had a hard day at work.* It's just easier to prop up on that crutch than to check in with the truth that you aren't getting it done at the office lately.

Think about it for a minute. You have behavior patterns that are directly impacting your life, and you've never viewed them as habits. In fact, you've probably never thought about them at all.

Maybe it's something like . . .

Partying. Going out. Drinking too much. When the weekend hits, it's just what you do. You go out with your friends, drink a few cocktails, and see where the night takes you. You say to yourself, *We're just having fun. Nobody is getting hurt. It's not a big deal.* But it's a behavioral pattern. You would never tell somebody, "I just want you to know that I'm a particr." But if they were to look at the pattern of your life, they would see partying is something you do with total consistency.

Are you stuck in it? I don't know. Maybe you are, maybe you're not. But it is a consistent pattern. And if you were honest with yourself about it, you'd say it's not healthy. You'd say you go out a lot, sometimes when you don't really want to, because it's easier than staying at home and spending time doing something more productive. It's easier than confronting or admitting your real loneliness.

Maybe your crutch is being less than honest. And if you called it what it really was, it'd be lying. Bending the truth a little in your favor. Maybe you've become so used to twisting the truth a little bit, it's something you do without thinking. You leave out some details. You edit. You change the story enough to keep yourself out of trouble. Or maybe you do it to make your life seem more interesting. It's just a reflex for you now. It's not lying; it's just how you tell stories. And you do it because there's something *untrue* you believe about yourself. There's something you're convinced that's missing from you or your life that other people have. And without telling a few "white lies" here and there, you may not be as exciting, or accepted, or loved.

Or your crutch is attention from men. Or women, whichever you're interested in. Maybe you browse your many dating apps every night or visit certain sites. Or maybe you just hit up people you know who will tell you what you want to hear. You spend hours texting and chatting, knowing the relationship will never get beyond that. You tell yourself it's not a big deal: *When I'm married, I'm not going to do this anymore.* Or maybe you don't even realize it's become a crutch; it's just part of your routine. If you were to really check in with the truth behind all these flirtations, you'd say that unless you have someone interested in you romantically, you aren't content with who you are.

How about comparing your life to other people's lives? Man, this will get even the best-intentioned person. This one you really have to guard against. Because no matter where you look, there's always going to be someone who looks like they got more than you got.

This is something I've had to stay away from my entire career, and I can't say I've always been successful. But in my industry, the temptation to compare is a way of life. It's a way of business. You're always doing it. *This album did better than this one. She got more solo shots than I did. Why is she getting credit for saying "Hit me!" on "Lose My Breath" when it's me who says it?!* You're always comparing where you are, who you are, and how you're doing based on the people around you.

Comparison can also become a crutch to us when we look at other people's lives to feel better about our own. "Well, at least I didn't get wasted at the neighborhood barbeque." But this habit is just as harmful. It lessens our level of accountability with ourselves because just like there's always going to be someone doing better than us, there's always going to be someone worse off than us. If we're only living to be better—or worse—than someone else, it's not a lifestyle of checking in.

Maybe it's gossip. Maybe it's a food addiction or eating disorder. Maybe it's talking negatively about yourself to the point where you just really don't like who you are. These crutches have become a way of life for you. They're patterns of behavior. They're habits. And they're what's keeping you from being able to check in.

Here's a question for you. Have you ever used actual crutches before? The kind with the rubber handles that go beneath your armpits? Well, I've never actually broken my leg or foot before, but I have played with a set of crutches. I was about seven or eight, and I was fooling around with a set that belonged to somebody in my family. After an afternoon of playing, I noticed something. My whole body hurt. Baaaby. I still remember the sting! Especially under my armpits and on my sides where the rubber was rubbing my skin raw.

Yeah, those crutches were fun at first. I probably would have gotten some extra attention if I'd used them in the grocery store or at school. But the truth is, crutches get old quick. Because they're not meant to be used forever.

Checking in will require many things of us, and one of the hardest of those is to put down our crutches. We may feel the chafed skin and the sore bones and walk a little unsteady at first. But if we reach within ourselves, within our circles, and within our faith, we will find life on our own two feet to be the most rewarding, healthiest choice we've ever made.

Chapter Ten

MY FIRST REAL FIGHT WAS AT CHURCH. MAKES sense, since my first kiss was at church too. I don't know, maybe I spent *too* much time in the Lord's house because apparently I was very comfortable having all my milestone moments there.

It was Vacation Bible School one summer, and this girl and I were walking out of the sanctuary, getting mouthy with each other. Whatever the argument was about, I'm sure it was dumb, but we were heated. So out of nowhere, she reached up and yanked me back by my ponytail. Then the Devil himself came up out of me.

I turned around and I laid a punch on that poor girl's face that I didn't even know I was capable of. About three seconds later, my older cousin Lynn, who had witnessed the whole thing, came out and verbally ripped us to absolute shreds. We both got right quick and shook hands with each other, and that was it. It was squashed. We never spoke of it again.

I wish forgiveness were that easy every time. But unfortunately, it's not.

Growing up, I was always one of those "neutral" girls. I wasn't really an athlete, or a drama kid, or a smart kid. I was a little bit of everything. I could be friends with two separate groups who were upset with each other. If I saw you in the hallway, I'd say hey no matter who you had beef with. I just stayed out of it as much as possible and played it cool with everybody. For the most part, I sort of kept to myself. But when I was in the fourth grade at Macintosh Elementary, I had my first experience being bullied.

I don't even know what made these certain two girls take a disliking to me, but they sure had no use for me. They would follow me to the bathroom to scare me, make comments about my teeth and my hair. They'd bump shoulders against me while walking down the hall or "fall" into me. I remember being really scared, actually. I didn't know from one day to the next if *today* was the day they were going to bash my head into the sink or something.

I remember being so confused. Like, *Why me?* What had I done to put myself on their radar? To become their target? Because I couldn't think of anything. I think that's what bothered me more than anything, that I had no control over the situation because I had been randomly singled out for their amusement.

Then one day my fears were realized. It started off in the lunchroom, and they were pretending to like me. Really, really like me. Maybe it was how much I wanted to be liked or maybe I was just stupid, but I believed them. I was like, "Oh, y'all are my friends today? That's so nice! That's so good. Glad you got over that whole we-hate-Michelle thing!"

So we walked out on the playground and I was just bouncing around because I was so happy they'd finally accepted me. We walked, and walked, and walked, and walked. And when we were as far away from the school as possible, the two girls jumped me. I fell to my knees on the freezing cold ground, more surprised by their sneak attack than actually injured. Being all of ten years old, their fighting skills consisted mostly of pushing my face into the snow and calling me names I won't repeat here.

"I can't breathe!" I yelled, lying. "I can't breathe!" And immediately they let me up. You'll never believe what they did next. Those heifers helped me off the ground and rushed me to the nurse's office.

They were all, "Oh, we were just playing. We were joking with Tenitra and then she couldn't breathe!"

I just went along with it until the (wise) nurse sent them out of the room and asked me what had really happened. When I told her, I felt instant relief and burst into tears. I hadn't realized how much tension I'd been carrying around until that moment. Not just about that particular incident, but about how much those girls hated me in general.

I never told my parents about what was going on, but you can't sneak anything past my mama. I'd had physical symptoms of anxiety that entire school year: loss of appetite, throwing up for no reason, slacking grades. But after the jumping incident, I couldn't deny what was going on anymore. I finished out the year at Macintosh, but my mom made sure a teacher escorted me from the school to the car every time I was picked up or dropped off. I wasn't to be left alone.

The next year she moved me to a different school. I didn't see those girls again until the seventh grade. And you know what? They were still up to the same shenanigans. I remember even being in high school and one of their sisters came into the department store I worked at, and I about hit the deck to hide from her. What if she'd brought her evil sibling in with her? I lived in a lot of fear of those girls. And for what? I'd done nothing wrong.

When I think back on that situation, I'm always shocked. As bad as those girls were to me, I was never angry with them. I was never mad at them. I was confused, but I always sort of knew that there had to be more going on than I understood. To this day, I've never held a grudge against them. Honestly, I want to cross paths with them and ask them, "Who hurt you girls? Were you being abused at home? Were you being bullied by someone older than us?" One of the girls looked like a grown woman when we were ten, so I bet she had someone picking on her and teasing her all the time.

That's the thing about forgiveness that trips me up sometimes—it doesn't get easier as you get older like so many other difficult things. No, forgiveness gets *harder*. I don't know if it's because the offenses get greater or our hearts get harder, but I've experienced unforgiveness in my own life, and it's a killer to mental health. I mean, it'll eat you up if you let it. Drive you mad. I actually believe that harboring unforgiveness can make you physically sick. Or even worse, it can keep you from reaching your full potential in your ministry and in your life.

I bet if we were to all check in with God and with those wounded places in our hearts, we'd find a few examples of people we need to forgive.

There's a lot of things I've learned about forgiveness:

- Forgiveness frees you.
- You've got to give forgiveness to get it.
- Forgiveness doesn't mean the person you're forgiving did nothing wrong.

You've probably heard all those things before. I have, and they're all true. But one thing no one told me about forgiveness is that it can take time. For one, there are natural consequences in your relationship when someone has hurt you. There's going to be distance. There's going to be less trust. There's going to be pain. You can't just look at the person and say, "I forgive you," and everything go back to normal. I think that's why I struggled with forgiving certain people for so long. Because I thought I had to *feel* a certain way to forgive them.

But forgiveness doesn't come with a feeling because it's not a feeling. Forgiveness is an action. It's something that's done. Sometimes it's easy. Sometimes it's hard. Sometimes it's something you have to say out loud. Sometimes it's something you have to scream inside your own heart over and over again. But it's not something you're going to necessarily relate to emotionally.

Another part of forgiveness that has always been confusing for me is the "after" part. Like, are we gonna hug and pretend we're cool again like me with the girl I fought? I don't want to be made a fool. That's something I probably care too much about. I don't want to be taken advantage of. And sometimes in my line of work, it's hard to know who is there for *you*, not for what you can give them. Maybe you've experienced that too. But I've been burned many times by people who were here for the party and not for the hostess.

So it's been challenging for me to separate withholding forgiveness from protecting myself. But one thing I've learned is that you can cut someone out of your life and still forgive them. Being a forgiving person doesn't mean you have to be a dumb person too.

Here's how I see it. When we hold a grudge against someone, we rehearse what they did to us over and over again in our heads. *She said that, he didn't do this.* Whatever it was, we replay the injury to ourselves like a movie reel. We feel like that person owes us something. Maybe it's an apology. But it's usually a lot more than that. And forgiveness simply takes that debt and cancels it out. It says, *You don't owe me anything. The ledger is clear. I release you.*

I may not *feel* all warm and fuzzy for you. I may even decide that I just don't like you. But you don't owe me anything, because I forgive you. I acknowledge the brokenness inside you. I acknowledge my side of the injury. I acknowledge that I'm not without blame in this life. Now, this may take days, weeks, months, even years. Forgiveness is almost always a process. But the more you recognize your own humanity, your own faults, your own shortcomings, the easier it is to empathize with others and offer them genuine forgiveness.

I mean, consider the alternative. Walking around holding grudges doesn't really feel good. Because it costs us something. It costs us time, energy, relationships. Holding grudges ain't free.

Do you know how they hunt monkeys in South America? They take a hollowed-out coconut, and they put a little hole in the side of it. The hole is big enough for a monkey to get a finger or two in, but not their whole hand. Then they take that hole, and they fill it with some kind of bait, like a piece of fruit. Then they hang that fruit-filled coconut from a tree.

So the monkey comes along and he sees the fruit. He's a hungry monkey and that fruit smells good, so he grabs it. But then he can't get his hand back out, because the hole is too small now that he's holding on to the fruit. Now, our monkey friend has a choice: either keep holding on to the fruit and stay trapped or let go of it and be free.

What do you think most monkeys do? They keep holding on, and *bam*! Done. They're now the property of a monkey hunter.

That's how a grudge works—the more you hold on to it, the more it has a hold on you. And when we refuse to let go of something we're mad about or we want to get back at someone about, we're the ones who suffer. We're the ones who become trapped.

I mean, think about how ridiculous it is. We think if we let go of that grudge, we're going to miss out on something. What's that about? What are we going to miss out on? Staying mad? Staying stuck? It doesn't even make sense. Most of the time our offender doesn't even know they've hurt us or to what extent. So we're not hurting them by holding on to our grudge. Our grudge isn't keeping them up at night; it's keeping us up at night. It's not slowing down their success, but it is hindering ours. Staying mad at an ex won't stop them from moving on to the next relationship, but it will prevent you from doing the same.

Look, even if you have no real desire to forgive someone else, be selfish enough to do it for you.

But there's another side to this whole topic, isn't there? It makes us uncomfortable to think about, so we are hesitant to check in about it. At least, not in a way that produces any action on our part. Not unless we're in a twelve-step program or a Bible study. It's the people that *we* need to ask for forgiveness. The people we've wronged along the way. And I'm not talking about just throwing out an, "I'm sorry about whatever went down between us, we cool?" but an actual heartfelt, specific apology.

Remember Anthony? The guy I dated and flipped out on before Chad? Turns out I did that more than once after that first incident at his place. Turns out I started a pattern (which I continued with Chad) of masquerading my hurt and insecurity as rage. And I hurt him. I knew I had, but I had never really asked him for forgiveness.

I was checking in with myself not too long ago and checking in with God too. And I was asking who had been injured by the shrap-nel of one of my depressive explosions, and Anthony's name came to mind. So I invited him to come out to the last day of a retreat I was on. He and I had remained friends, so this wasn't the craziest thing I'd ever asked of him. He agreed. I remember when he got there, I was in the kitchen cooking for some of the other ladies. I still had my apron on and everything. But as soon as I saw him, I knew I had to ask for his forgiveness. It had started weighing on me, and I knew it was the Holy Spirit telling me it was time.

I surprised myself when I burst into tears. Like I've said, I'm not much of a crier. It was one of those cries that's already happening by the time you realize it. So I just started talking. I was like, "I need to ask you to forgive me. My responses to you were not always kind or good."

Anthony, bless him, was not expecting all that. He was like, "Michelle, you said you were sorry years ago. It's okay." But it wasn't. I knew it wasn't because I felt it. I had said I was sorry, but I hadn't asked for forgiveness.

Ideally, when you ask for forgiveness, do it face-to-face. If at all possible, do it in person. There's just something about seeing some-one's heart through their eyes, their expressions, their presence in the room—it communicates things that words can't. Also, use specific examples of what you did wrong. That's going to be uncomfortable—maybe for both of you—but general apologies don't mean as much as the ones that name the wrong. If you're not sure exactly what you did to hurt them, ask! Ask, then repeat back what they said and ask for forgiveness. It's not going to come naturally or feel great, but it releases you. It releases both of you.

Sometimes the hardest person to forgive is yourself. After my last breakup with Chad, I thought I'd never be able to look myself in the face again. In my family, I'm known for three things: not being able to cook, not being able to drive, and not being able to keep a man. And just as much as I hated letting down Chad, I hated letting them down. Because they had been cheering for me—cheering for *us*. They were so excited and filled with joy that Chad and I had found each other. Then I went and put that dream in a shredder. My dream, Chad's dream, their dream, ribbons of wrinkled and ink-stained paper, hopelessly thin and useless.

If I had been the only person hurt, it wouldn't have been as hard to forgive myself. But hurting the man I loved and the people I loved . . . the shame was deafening. It was all I could hear.

I would say that today, I am still working to forgive myself for my behavior in past relationships. I get it from my mom, my ability to wound with my words. I have a magnet from Hobby Lobby that says, "Sometimes when I open my mouth, my mom comes out." My mother could write you a ten-page letter in about ten minutes, and it'd be so eloquent and articulate. She is very intelligent. But baaaby, you do not want to be on the receiving end of Mrs. Williams's anger.

Let me give you an example. She's going to die when she reads this, but she put it on Twitter and half the world has already seen it. One time I was getting just worn out by this Twitter user. I mean, they were saying some nasty things. Just really being derogatory about my talent and my character. Granted, this person didn't know me from a stranger on a street corner. I had heard about some of the things they had written, but I had chosen to ignore it.

My mama, on the other hand, was not feeling so amenable. At all. She got online, and do you know what she typed and published for all the internet to read? She replied to one of this user's comments and said, "Your parents should have wiped you up with a tissue."

I mean, I could have died. I wasn't really embarrassed; I thought it was sort of funny. But I was just shocked my mama talked like that. The sex talk she had with my sister and me was all of one sentence. We were getting ready for church one day, and she walked in and said, "Don't y'all be out there having sex. You'll get too attached."

That was it! So for her to come out on Twitter swinging with words like those, I was like, "Mama. You can't say stuff like that." She didn't care. She was sticking up for her baby.

So yeah, I come by my pop-offs real honest. And looking back at my relationship with Chad, I still hate what I did. But I don't hate who I am. In the past, I've been so bad about shouldering all the blame myself. Because I exploded, it was all my fault. But that's an oversimplification. In any relationship, there are two people feeding off each other's energy and vibes and habits. I didn't melt down all by myself out of nowhere; though, I will admit I handled myself poorly. I acknowledge my role, but I acknowledge Chad's too.

I can separate my mental illness from the person I really am and see how sick I allowed myself to get. I can see the fault in my actions but not the innate fault in *me*. But that took time. A lot of time, a lot of prayer, and a lot of therapy. A lot of checking in.

When you think about it, you have no choice but to forgive yourself. There's nothing you can do to take whatever you're ashamed of back. The only thing that will help is time to rebuild your trust in yourself. The same goes for when you ask somebody else for forgiveness.

When I apologized to Anthony, I had no idea what his response was going to be. And that was good. You can't write a script for how you think the person you're approaching is going to react. Honestly, you can't have any expectations whatsoever. You can't have any motives or agenda outside of offering your apology. You can't go into it hoping to get something in return. True contrition is a sacrifice, not an exchange.

You may not get an ending like Anthony and I had. Or you may get it, but it might take some time.

Sometime in 2019, I worked up the courage to truly ask Chad for forgiveness. And he didn't immediately forgive me. I think he wanted to, but it's hard when someone has done something to you more than once to believe they're not going to do that same thing again. And it's hard when someone has truly wronged you. Like, I didn't deserve his forgiveness. I had hurt him. I had humiliated him and rejected him. And no matter how bad he may have wanted things to go right back to how they were, they couldn't.

There's a difference between reconciliation and restoration. Reconciliation is when you both offer and accept forgiveness. Restoration is when the relationship is fulfilled. Either to its previous status or maybe even something deeper. But if you go into any apology seeking restoration, you're setting yourself up for disappointment.

For Chad, it took a few months for that ice to melt. I had to give him time *and* space from me. That wasn't easy. I don't like it when people are upset with me or hurt by me. But at that point, I realized that all I could do was continue to check in. To work on me. All I could do was ask God to heal me, change me, and forgive me. And I had to trust that the Holy Spirit would work on Chad's heart toward me, even though we weren't really in contact with one another.

You may have to do something like that; you may have to give someone space after you ask for their forgiveness. Think about wounds, physical wounds. The worse they are, the longer they take to get better. The ones where there's bone exposed and the flesh is torn? You can't pop a little Neosporin on those and go about your business. No, the healing takes more time and energy. Now, if the offense is a scratch? Somebody forgot a birthday. Somebody spoke out of turn. Those don't take as long.

But you know, I'm looking at my bare knees right now, and there are still scars from my scrapes. The skin is all closed up and nothing is broken, but I can still see where I got hurt.

There's one from a time I fell off a bike trying to go down a hill too fast. It left a huge Y-shaped scar. When I look at it, I don't feel pain anymore. I don't even really remember it. Then I've got another one on my shin from where I fell in a haunted house. I have no business being at haunted houses because they absolutely terrify me.

I want to try to be that same way when it comes to forgiving others. This is especially important in relationships with family. Because you can't un-family family. I'll think I've forgiven a family member, and then they'll say something, and then I have to forgive them for everything they've ever done or said to hurt me all over again. Like, I have to start my forgiveness journey with them at the very beginning.

See, I'm still not "there" yet. Not fully when it comes to checking in with the unforgiveness in my heart. But I want to get there. When I think about what happened to me, I want to remember the incident but not relive the pain. Like, "Man, I was a dumb butt riding down the hill like I was on the Tour de France. That was so stupid." Or, "Yup. That was the time that zombie jumped out and scared me. That one was my fault. I knew that was a bad idea. I kind of deserve that scar." And leave it at that.

Because the thing is, I'm going to keep jacking up. I know I will. I am sure that one day I will irritate the dog out of my husband. I will need his forgiveness. And if we want it, we have to give it.

One of my favorite questions from the Bible came from a guy named Peter. He was one of Jesus' closest friends and followers. One day, they were all kicking it, and Peter went up to Jesus and was like, "So, how do we know when to forgive?"

Don't you do that with your parents? Or didn't you when you were growing up? You have a specific situation in mind, and you don't really want to go into detail, so you ask a general question like that. Like, "Hypothetically, Jesus, let's say someone has wronged me. How would I go about handling that?"

I bet Peter had a person or a situation in mind. Maybe he had gotten into another argument with his brother Andrew. Maybe the government was doing him dirty. Maybe someone had called him a derogatory name or term. We don't know the situation; all we know is that Peter wanted answers: "Then Peter came to Jesus and asked, 'Lord, how many times shall I forgive my brother or sister who sins against me? Up to seven times?'" (Matthew 18:21 NIV).

First, Peter wasn't talking about his actual brother or sister. He was talking about anybody—any man, woman, ex, parent, teacher, boss, or friend who might hurt him.

Second, Jewish law actually limited the number of times you

forgave someone. After three, you didn't have to forgive them anymore. So Peter, obviously trying to impress Jesus and his friends, decided to go ahead and bump that number up to seven. He's like, *I'm willing to double that Jewish law plus one.*

I see you, Pete! Out there trying to one-up your friends in front of Jesus.

Jesus was so cool, though. He didn't get flustered or roll his eyes. He's like, "Seven's a good number. But what about seventy times seven?" (v. 22, my paraphrase).

Now, if you've ever heard this scripture preached, you've probably heard this; Jesus wasn't giving a literal number. Jesus wasn't saying, "Do the math! Then stop forgiving!" Jesus was basically saying that Peter wasn't asking the right question. Peter didn't understand the concept of forgiveness. It's not a feeling. It's not something you do because you want to. It's not even something you do because God told you to. It's something you do to live the best version of your life.

Being able to forgive others, ask for forgiveness, and forgive yourself is about *you.* It's about checking in with your heart and not being tied to someone in a negative way.

Jesus was so serious about forgiveness that he modeled it for us to the greatest extreme. How far should we go? When should we forgive? What is it worth? Jesus went so far as to give up his life. He exchanged his life for the dirty rags of our sins just so we could experience God's complete forgiveness.

And if you've never heard that before, it is my genuine honor to say it: Jesus died for you. For everything you've done and everything you will do. When he looks at you, he doesn't see the screwups, the

Being able
to forgive
others, ask for
forgiveness, and
forgive yourself
is about you. It's
about checking in
with your heart
and not being
tied to someone
in a negative way.

mistakes, the failures. He sees perfection. He sees someone worth saving. Someone worth dying for.

And if you've never checked in with Jesus and asked him to be a bigger part of your life, asked him to forgive you, asked him to be your Savior, I pray right now that you'd do that.

Talk about a check-in to remember!

Chapter Eleven

GOD'S GOT JOKES. NO, HE DOES. I'M TELLING YOU,
sometimes I imagine him up there on his throne sort of laughing to
himself like, "Yo. Just when she's comfortable, I'm gonna kinda pull out
the rug under her feet just a little bit and remind her she needs me."

Because if God doesn't tap me on the shoulder every now and
then, I will start thinking I can do this thing on my own. And by "this
thing," I mean life. My entire life. So—God's got jokes *and* infinite
knowledge of his children.

The thing about writing a book is that I started this process long
before you added my title to your cart. (Thanks for that, by the way!)
And somewhere in my editing journey, I found myself in the middle of
both a global pandemic and a war on racism in America.

I had a choice to make: Do I send to print what I had already written without acknowledging these two culture-altering events, or do I
go back to work?

It really wasn't even a choice, to be honest. Because never in the
history of the world has there ever been a more crucial time for us to
be checking in.

When I first heard about Covid-19, I was in Los Angeles for award
show season. It was a really exciting time in my life because I was gear-
ing up for a huge tour that would launch at the end of May and run
through August. I was going to be on stage again, be an *artist* again.
So I was taking meetings with agents and spending time with my girls.
It felt like something *big* was about to start for me. Something *new*.

I remember getting ready for a Grammys after-party and hearing about the virus as it spread through different parts of the world. And like many Americans at the time, I wasn't at all worried for myself or my country. While I did have genuine concern for my international brothers and sisters who were struggling, I was guilty of having a "that'll never spread here" mentality.

Fast-forward to March 2020 and I was serving at a retreat in North Carolina (the same one I attended that changed my life!). It was like the world was one way when the week started and completely different when the week ended. News outlets were cranking out stories that the coronavirus was in the United States and it wasn't going anywhere. Folks were wilding out over toilet paper, and I was like, *toilet paper*? Y'all know about washcloths, right? I mean, I'm not trying to get rude, here. But *toilet paper*?

I knew I only had about four rolls to my name, so just like y'all probably did, I stopped at the grocery store on my way home to Atlanta. And I got everything (that I could). Chips, Oreos, kombucha, ground beef, chicken wings, fruit snacks. I mean, I went bonkers. And boy am I glad I did, because I didn't leave my place for the next twelve days. Then the Italian restaurant down the street opened up for takeout, and I'd hop in my car with my mask on and pick up a calzone and some tiramisu just to hunker down again.

Y'all know that I'm used to living alone. I've lived alone forever and I don't mind it. So when I heard we were all being asked to stay home, I was like, *done and done*. But living in a world under quarantine is not how God created us to live. After a while, I was like, *Oh no. This is gonna be bad. I'm going to get depressed. What if I spiral?*

But you know what? I didn't.

I'm an outdoors person—especially when the weather is nice. So instead of sitting inside, watering that initial seed of fear, I went outside. I took walks by the river. I moved my body. I breathed in fresh air. You know, there are a lot of drugs out in the world that I don't know much about, but what I can tell you is that a little outdoor oxygen can hit you *just right*.

During these walks, I didn't listen to anything. I listened to myself. I asked myself tough questions like, "Are you in this moment? Or trying to get through this moment? Are you avoiding your real feelings because you might get scared? Or are you really okay?"

It wasn't until I sat down to tell you about my Covid experience that I even realized it . . . y'all—I was checking in! I was checking in with *me* during these walks. I was processing my thoughts, feelings, and actions. And I was lining it all up to the Word. I calmed any sort of anxious thoughts by remembering, "God is with you. God is with his children. This will pass."

But don't get it twisted—there were still some hard moments for me. I was super disappointed that certain business opportunities were being postponed or cancelled. I was looking forward to getting back to work touring again. I was looking forward to taking trips. This was the year that I said, "I'm going to travel more than ever. Even if I have to go by myself."

And coronavirus said, "Whomp, whomp!"

But through checking in with myself, that disappointment didn't turn into anxiety. It's okay to be disappointed. But God doesn't want us to live in fear.

Now, when it came to checking in with others during Covid, I had to be a little more intentional. Because I'm such an introvert, this is always going to be the hardest piece of the checking-in puzzle for me to get into place.

Communication during quarantine probably looked the same for me as it did for a lot of you. A lot of FaceTime. A lot of texting. Everybody was on social media all the livelong day. I've been on more Zoom meetings than I can count, and I will *never* complain about hopping on a plane for a meeting again!

But here's one thing I've learned about people while checking in during Covid—everyone feels like *they're* the one doing all the checking in. And I get like this too. I feel like I'm the one making all the effort in certain relationships. But what I have failed to understand in the past is that you might be the only one initiating conversations with certain people. In other words, they're doing all the reaching out in all their other relationships, but you—you're the one friend who makes the first move with them.

The other thing the quarantine taught me about checking in with others is that I don't do enough of it. I assume that if I'm not hearing from you, everything is fine. "No news is good news." But that's not always the case; it certainly hasn't always been the case with me. I've learned to even look for the friends who have gone sort of "radio silent," either online or over the phone. And I'll just send them a quick message. Nothing indicting like, "You've been quiet, are you okay?" But something inviting: "Hey, friend. Just thinking of you."

What I'm trying to say is, if it crosses your mind to reach out to someone to check in with them, don't hesitate. Don't check the scorecard to see who has texted or called more. Don't assume anything. Just do it. You may have to move out of your comfort zone when it comes to checking in with others. I don't like to bother people, and I don't particularly like to be bothered. But there were several people who reached out to me during the Covid crisis that made me think, *Wait, what? You like me? You care enough to take the time to say something to me?* People I hadn't heard from in ages. I learned I need to get off my Recently Called list and open up my Contacts and ask, "Who needs to hear from me right now?"

For me, the easiest check-in of the quarantine was checking in with God. I'm telling you, honey, I was praying without even knowing it. I'd be in the middle of a thought and realize it was a prayer. *God, when I come out of this, I want to be stronger. I want to have a better heart. I want to be more loving and more compassionate than ever before.*

It felt like I was surrounded by people who were hurting. Makeup artist friends, hairdresser friends, athlete friends—all out of work for the foreseeable future. I also have a cousin who works the ER at a big city hospital. He was on the frontlines. I have always respected those in the medical field, but the coronavirus made their sacrifice very personal for me. I learned to intercede for people—to check in with God for others—like never before.

Right now, I'm sitting on my sofa staring at my plants. House plants—that was something I got into during the quarantine. They've become like children to me. And I've got this orchid in front of me that's just giving me the blues. It needs a lot of attention—more attention than my other plant children. I imagine this orchid is a lot like me. Stubborn. Moody. Unpredictable. And yet, it still grows. It still lives. And it still blossoms. Just as our communities, country, and world will continue to do—one bloom at a time, all in God's time.

∽

Y'all didn't think I was going to leave you hanging on that Chad front, did you? I wouldn't do you like that. Because if I were you, I'd be wondering: What's the story now? How am I doing? How is Chad doing?

Let me check in with you one last time . . . for now.

I was walking to my apartment not too long ago, and my sweet little neighbor stopped me in the hallway. She's the most adorable little Asian grandma you've ever seen. I mean, just precious. She said, "Do you live here alone?"

I had just gotten back from a baby shower for a friend of mine. She's my age, her tiny belly just poking out so cute and little.

"Yes, ma'am, I do live alone," I told her.

She looked confused. "Why don't you have a husband?"

I almost had one, but my depression ran him off.

I went inside and got settled into my place, all by myself. But I wasn't sad.

A year ago, her question would have bothered me. It would have hurt. Coming fresh from a baby shower, her words probably would have ruined the night, back in the day. But I looked around my apartment and I felt content. I checked in with the facts:

- I've got friends to love on and celebrate with.
- I've got a nice home to live in that I can afford all on my own.
- My Asian neighbor is confused by my singleness.

Now that I'm checking in, I can do this. I can accept my reality and still hope in God's promises for my future without letting either control my moods and reactions.

I mean, isn't that really a compliment? That she didn't take one look at me and say, "No wonder you're single, sis! You're ugly and old and tired!"

Now that I'm checking in, I can do this. I can accept my reality and still hope in God's promises for my future without letting either control my moods and reactions. (Most days, I'm still human.)

As for Chad and me, we are in touch. Just before the quarantine began in 2020, I watched online as he preached to a packed house for the first time in a year. See, Chad has been checking in too. He's been working on himself and asking himself tough questions as well. He's been surrounding himself with the right people and bringing his issues to God and asking for help.

As I watched him teach, I was just boo-hooing.

You know the feeling you get when you see a professional athlete doing their thing? In their element? Doing what only they can do? That's how I felt watching Chad. Teaching people about God's love is what Chad is meant to do in this life.

A lot of our conversations right now are simply processing. I'm listening to what he was thinking and feeling over the course of our time together. I continue to offer him my apologies. He's working so hard. But there was a lot of hurt. And that kind of forgiveness takes time.

It's a journey. Whatever comes next, I want it to be directly from the hand of God. I feel him in the middle of it. I don't know what he's doing, but he's at work. He's in this, making something beautiful out of something tragic.

And that's not just true for me. It's true for you too. I hope you feel empowered. Especially if you suffer from mental illness or depression,

I hope I've given you one or two tools to throw in your toolbox for the next time the dark clouds roll in.

I hope that you've laughed, reading this book. Lord knows I've laughed at myself. I hope you also felt a little challenged—challenged to check in with whatever area of your life is weighing you down. But more than all those things, I hope you know you're not alone in the fight. Whether or not you have depression, we all have struggles. We all go through hard times. I want you to know that life isn't singling you out. God isn't singling you out.

If nothing else, maybe I've given you some language to use. I hope you've read something here that allows you to ask for help when you need it from the right people. Maybe you've seen some scripture that you can commit to memory or read a prayer that you can pray over your life. I also hope some of y'all can get some reconciliation *and* restoration in your lives. Maybe that's with family members, friends, coworkers, whoever. Not everybody has a list of exes they need to make amends with. Not everybody has left a path of relational destruction like I have. Then again, maybe you have. And that's okay. But now it's time to do something about it.

I just want you to feel like you can make it. I want you to *know* you can make it.

I want you to trust God.

I trust God. I trust the people in my life I've invited in to be part of my circle. And for the first time in my life, I finally trust myself.

This is a place I can only get to by checking in.

If I could leave you with any word of advice, it'd be this: *Hold on.*

Wherever you are, whoever you are, whatever you've done, whatever's been done to you, *hold on.*

Because God isn't finished with your story yet. He's about to flip the page and take your journey a different direction. But you'll miss it if you don't hold on.

When your depression flattens you, your anxiety consumes you, and your pain rages against your senses, *hold on*.

Tell those voices in your head, the ones echoing the opinions of a few or the ones that just love to nag you and degrade you, tell those voices to shut up. Nah, tell them to shut the *hell* up.

Open your Bible to Philippians 4:8 and *hold on* to the words there:

Finally, believers, whatever is true, whatever is honorable and worthy of respect, whatever is right and confirmed by God's word, whatever is pure and wholesome, whatever is lovely and brings peace, whatever is admirable and of good repute; if there is any excellence, if there is anything worthy of praise, think continually on these things [center your mind on them, and implant them in your heart].

Replace the lies with truth.
Trust in the character of God.
Hold on.
And check in.

Acknowledgments

TO THE FRIENDS, FAMILY, COLLEAGUES, AND ORGANIZATIONS who have taught me how to check in, *thank you*. Thank you for inspiring me. For loving me. For checking in with me and being people I can check in with too. Without you this book would not exist. You have filled my life with hope, with joy, but more importantly, you have filled my life with truth. Thank you to:

- Trent and Brittany Phillips
- Wale and Dr. Amira Ogunleye
- Jonathan Azu
- Pastor Toure and Sarah Roberts
- Dr. Tara Jenkins
- Pastor Mike and Dr. Dee Dee Freeman
- Pastor Phil and Emily Manginelli
- Kelly Rowland
- Beyoncé Carter
- Tina Knowles Lawson
- Lee and Denise Boggs

- Annie Kelahan, my therapist
- Chad Johnson
- Dr. Caroline Leaf
- Pastors Jeremy and Jenny DeWeerdt

My family and my friends who have become family. You are my people—you are my tribe!

To Jenny Baumgartner and my amazing team at HarperCollins Christian and Nelson Books who helped make this book possible, thank you. It has been a JOY working with you. I miss our weekly virtual meetings already.

Thank you, Dr. Holly Carter. Everything that I have voiced to you that I've wanted to do—you've helped to make it all happen.

To my amazing agent Whitney Gossett, thank you for your belief in me throughout the years.

Holly Crawshaw, the fun we had putting this book together became the start of something beautiful. I'm so thankful for you! More cream cheese brownies!

My Sunshine, none other than Yvette Noel Schure, I love you so much.

God, I thank you for all that you've brought me through. I thank you for showing me life truly is worth living just because you live, and you live inside of me!

I also want to acknowledge the life-giving organization of Mental Health America. If you or someone you know is experiencing thoughts of despair, depression, or suicide, please check in by checking out these resources:

- The National Alliance of Mental Health Institution: www.NAMI.org
- The National Suicide Prevention Hotline: 1-800-273-8255
- Healing Heart Retreat: www.livingwatersministry.com

Notes

Chapter 1

1. Tony Arevalo, "24+ Mental Health Statistics You Should Know (2020)," Policy Advice, April 22, 2020, https://policyadvice.net/health -insurance/insights/mental-health-statistics/.
2. Carol Leather and Eleanor, "How Long Should It Take Me to Embroider a Piece?" Needlework Tips and Techniques, https://www .needlework-tips-and-techniques.com/how-long-should-it-take-me-to -embroider-a-piece.html.

Chapter 4

1. Hart Ramsey (@hartramsey), "If you don't heal properly after leaving a dysfunctional relationship you will end up in a different version of the same relationship you just escaped from," Twitter, January 23, 2020, 6:08 p.m., https://twitter.com/hartramsey /status/1220498469640720388.

Chapter 5

1. Colleen Vanderlinden, "It's True—You Really Should Talk to Your Plants," *The Spruce*, https://www.thespruce.com /should-you-talk-to-your-plants-3972298.

About the Author

MICHELLE WILLIAMS IS A GRAMMY AWARD-WINNING recording artist and actress who rose to stardom as a member of the R&B mega group, Destiny's Child, and most recently appeared as the Butterfly on Fox's hit series, *The Masked Singer*. Her successful solo albums include *Heart to Yours*; *Do You Know*; *Unexpected*, which spawned the internationally charted single, "We Break the Dawn"; and *Journey to Freedom*, which featured groupmates Beyoncé and Kelly Rowland on the single, "Say Yes." Also a talented actress, she debuted on Broadway in *Aida* (2003) and starred in productions of *The Color Purple* (2007), *Chicago* (2009–2010), *What My Husband Doesn't Know* (2011), and *Fela!* (2013). Michelle is passionate about raising awareness about mental health and about sharing the lessons she has learned in her own struggle with depression.